CW00400191

Fror
St James' Park
to
St James' Park

The story of my quest to see a match
at all of the
92 English Football League Grounds

by
Colin 'Podge' Harrison

Introduction

In July 2015, just after Newcastle's pre-season friendly at York City, I decided to check out how many football grounds I had watched a match at. The answer was 70, however only 58 of those were current football league grounds.

It was then, that I decided to actively go to games in order to complete 'The 92'. This would mean attending some 'random' games, as I knew this feat would not be possible just following Newcastle United.

What follows are my recollections of the days travelling up and down the country in order to reach my goal. It's a personal achievement, and one that will need to be revisited each time there is a new team promoted to the Football League, or whenever a team relocates to a new stadium. As you will read, I have attended well over 100 grounds to make this happen. I'm sure there will be more.

It is no coincidence that this story starts with my first trip in 1979 to St James' Park, Newcastle, and ends with a trip to the other St. James' Park, Exeter in 2018.

CHAPTER 1

The Early Years

13/11/79 – St. James' Park

At an early age I loved playing football. My house was next to a large open football field where, once I had started to walk, I would spend hours upon hours playing football with the other lads from our village. I was born into a Newcastle United family and my first hero was Malcolm Macdonald. I was upset as a five-year old when he left to sign for Arsenal, so much so that I recall looking for their results to see if SuperMac had scored that day before checking for Newcastle's score.

In 1979 Willie McFaul was granted a testimonial by Newcastle and the news was that SuperMac was going to play for Newcastle once again. I begged my parents to allow my older brother George, who usually went to the home games, to take me to my first ever game. It was agreed that I could go, but as it was a Tuesday evening game it would be difficult to get back home considering we lived just over 10 miles from the ground, and public transport was not the greatest. My Godmother's son, Malcolm 'Maxi' Turner, went to the matches with my brother. The good news was he could drive, and it was agreed this was to be my first visit to St James' Park.

I can remember putting on my scarf, and even tying one around my wrist so that I could wave it without the fear of losing my grip on a prized possession. I can recall sitting in the back seat of Maxi's car, and being laughed at for asking, what they called a silly question. 'Can you hear the commentator when the match is being played?' I asked. Considering I had only seen football on television, I didn't think this was a silly question at all...

I was taken to the Gallowgate end, to stand in front of the scoreboard, and this is where I would stand whenever I would return in the years to come. The turnstiles were marked 'Boys' and 'Men', the thought of a female in the crowd unheard of. I was ushered to the correct queue with the smell of the hops from the local brewery filling my nostrils. My brother paid the

3

man on the gate and pushed me through, telling me to wait at the other end as he had to go through a separate turnstile. I stood in awe as a huge policeman blocked my way, but I was rescued by my big brother within seconds. We climbed the steps, which seemed to go on forever, and then I saw it... The hallowed turf, the turf I dreamt about gracing, the turf I'd seen only on Match of the Day, and the turf where my heroes scored goals. The floodlights beamed brightly, but not as brightly as my wide open eyes. This was it; I was now a part of the Geordie faithful.

I recall the moment SuperMac ran onto the pitch, I cheered as loudly as I my eight year old lungs would let me. What happened next will stay with me forever. Malcolm Macdonald scored for Newcastle. I was there. I saw it. I don't remember much more about the game, but at half-time there was a penalty shoot-out which again captured my imagination. The game ended in a 4-1 win for Newcastle in front of just under 15,000 fans. It might have been Willie McFaul's testimonial but it was the greatest night of my life.

17/10/81 – Elland Road

Over the next few years, I used to play football at every opportunity. I was picked to play for my junior school team, and went on to be selected for the district side, Chester-le-Street Boys. In October 1981, we played away against a team from the Manchester area on a Saturday morning, and on the afternoon our whole squad were taken to watch a match that was taking place nearby. That match was Leeds United v West Bromwich Albion in Division One. The line ups included names such as John Lukic and Kenny Burns for Leeds, and David Mills and Cyrille Regis for West Brom. I had heard of these players from watching TV and reading The Pink every Saturday night. The game ended in a 3-1 home win with the highlight being the goal scored by Terry Connor for Leeds. He hit it from about 30 yards and it flew in.

16/4/82 – Edgeley Park

A tour of the Manchester area during the Easter holidays for Chester Boys meant we played three games in three days. This also meant we were taken to another ground to watch Stockport County play York City on a Friday night. This was a Division Four match and because of this I didn't know any of the names in either side. The attendance was less than 2,000 and Stockport ran out 4-1 winners.

9/5/87 – The City Ground

It was the last day of the season, and my brother asked if I fancied going with him to watch Newcastle play at Nottingham Forest. I was nearly 16, and this was my first Newcastle away match. Without much hesitation, I was quickly belted up in the back of the car heading south. The match itself was played on a bright sunny day. We were stood in the corner of the ground where some Newcastle fans were climbing up the floodlight. We went two goals down before halftime but the atmosphere was quite strange. The reason was Sunderland were losing at home which meant they were in a relegation playoff spot. This would see them fall into the third tier of English football. Paul 'Gazza' Gascoigne pulled one back for Newcastle in the second half but that was as good as it got. At the final whistle, the daft lads from the away end spilled onto the pitch. Actually, they didn't spill; they climbed the fences around the pitch to get there. There were a few local policemen trying to keep order, who were quite happily using their truncheons with accuracy, and with some effect as they connected with the fans hanging from the goalposts.

8/8/87 – Wembley Stadium (old)

Once again my big brother came up with the idea of visiting Wembley when it was announced The Football League would be holding a centenary match against The Rest of the World. The teams would be managed by Bobby Robson and Terry Venables, but the big attraction was that Diego Maradona would be playing. Just over 12 months previous, he was the most hated man in England when he punched the ball past Peter Shilton during The World Cup. Other names announced to play were Bryan Robson, Chris Waddle and Peter Beardsley for the 'home' team, and for the visitors were the likes of Michel Platini, Gary Lineker, Paulo Futre and the Brazilian, Josimar.

Just the thought of going to Wembley had me excited. I had watched every FA Cup Final that I could recall as a kid, dreaming about this stadium, and all the history that went with it. The game saw The Football League side run out 3-0 winners but two memories stick with me, which both took place during the halftime interval. Firstly, Pele was announced to the crowd and he made his way around the pitch waving to the 61,000 people inside. Everyone, including me who had only seen clips of this player on television lifting the World Cup and scoring wonderful goals, applauded the great man.

The next thing I remember was Diego Maradona walking to the centre circle by himself. Virtually the entire stadium, who had just been clapping Pele, started whistling, screaming, and shouting abuse at their biggest enemy. Maradona started to do a piece of ball juggling to show off his skills, and after two minutes without the ball touching the pitch, or even the player coming close to losing any control, the crowd's boos and jeers turned to applause. Fair play to him for even agreeing to play in such a game, so soon after the 'Hand of God' incident, shows a great deal of love for the game.

CHAPTER 2

Old Enough To Drink

24/9/89 – Roker Park

I had left school, found a job, fell in love with a girl who was to become my wife, and found out I was to become a father in a whirlwind couple of years. My girlfriend's brother-in-law Gary was a Mackem, but we got on due to our love of the game. He said we could go to the Sunderland-Newcastle derby match together and stand on the Fullwell End with the other Wearside fans. I asked my best mate Stephen Steele if he fancied and it was agreed we would go. There was a Sunderland supporters coach running from Stanley which was to be our mode of transport. We didn't wear any colours and thankfully the game ended 0-0 without any major incidents to get excited about. I cannot imagine doing that at these games now. These games have turned so hostile in recent years that it's become a military operation to get opposing fans in and out of the grounds.

23/1/90 – Ayresome Park

I became a dad on the 6th January 1990 on a day when Newcastle were playing away at Hull City in the FA Cup. Thankfully I hadn't planned to go there that day. I did think it would be a good idea to watch Newcastle play Middlesbrough in the Zenith Data Systems Cup on a Tuesday night. Stephen and I caught a bus to Durham then another to Middlesbrough arriving in the town centre around 6pm. What we weren't expecting was being chased by a group of skinheads who had stumbled out of a pub and recognised our accents were not from Teesside. We escaped without being caught and eventually arrived at the ground around an hour before kick-off. We hadn't really thought of how we were to get back home after the game, not fancying a walk to the bus station again. Newcastle lost 1-0 with the goal coming virtually on full time. Outside the ground were a number of buses which we just jumped on, hoping no-one would say anything. A few minutes later we were heading to Thornaby train station where a train would take us back to Newcastle. Sitting on the train the dreaded words of 'Tickets please' were shouted by the inspector walking down the aisle towards us. We informed him we didn't have one, and he told us we would need to pay the fine of £3.20. I think we had paid £3 to get to Middlesbrough so it wasn't too bad. We got into Central station and managed to catch the last bus to Chester le Street. Cash was now at a minimum so we could not afford a taxi. A long three mile walk at midnight in the cold of January is not recommended, however I was grateful to be home when my head hit the pillow around 1am.

24/2/90 – Bramall Lane

Stephen and I were now getting the buzz of an away trip and decided on a trip to promotion rivals Sheffield United. We were travelling on the supporter's bus, picking us up outside of the High Crown in Chester le Street. When we arrived around an hour before the game we were herded into the ground without any chance of a look around the Steel City.

Newcastle opened the scoring and looked to be heading for a huge victory before Brian Deane equalized with three minutes remaining. Standing on the terrace at this game, I heard one of the funny remarks you hear about players. Newcastle's winger that day was Wayne Fereday. The heckle he received was 'Fereday, you are fast, you are furious, but you are fucking shit'. Sadly, the guy who shouted it wasn't wrong.

30/11/91 – Oakwell

It was a little longer before my next ground was ticked off. Once again, Stephen and I chose Barnsley as our next destination. We managed to persuade another friend to come along, Gareth Donkin. Once again, we went by the supporter's bus.

We stood behind the goal on an open terrace with a huge drop at the back. The heavens opened at the same time as Newcastle's defence. Three-nil down at halftime, getting absolutely soaked wasn't what we had planned. The second half saw no more goals, but plenty more rain. We got back on the bus and sat in our wet jeans shivering all the way home.

5/12/92 – Meadow Lane

This season was turning out to be quite good for a Newcastle fan. Kevin Keegan had taken over and the club was heading for the Premier League. Gaz Donkin informed me that his mate was running a mini bus going to this game so I, along with Stephen and two of my work mates Graeme Vasey and Bryan Nixon were all up for it as well. The night before we all went to Chester le Street on the booze and it was quite a late one. On the way home Graeme and I were walking through the icy roads of South Stanley when we both went flying. We managed to make our way home ready to be picked up early the following day. I woke up with the worst hangover I have ever had, I walked to Graeme's to find him still asleep. He woke up and rushed out. I'm sure he was wearing the same clothes as last night. On the way, the effects of the booze were causing Graeme problems and he was about to throw up. Luckily the mini bus had a slide along window which he stuck his head out of as we were hurtling down the motorway. The side of the bus was not a pretty sight when we stopped at a nearby pub for the usual pre-match beers. The match was quite even in the first half and when the whistle blew Gaz, who was rather intoxicated, thought that was full time and headed for the exit. Newcastle scored just after half time and again just before full time to send the Geordie faithful home in high spirits. The trip home was quite eventful too. We stopped off for fish & chips somewhere, and this is when Bryan threw up. What came out of him was none stop. A huge dustbin lid sized pile of puke was splattered onto the pavement. Back on the bus, there was a horrible smell coming from the back. One of the lads had nicked the huge jar of pickled eggs from the fish shop counter. How anyone can eat those is beyond me.

13/3/93 – County Ground

Newcastle were flying high so we decided on a trip to Swindon Town. They were pushing for promotion themselves so we knew this wouldn't be an easy game. Bryan decided he would drive as long as Stephen and I chipped in for a hire car.

All three of us had just recently passed our driving test, but nothing could prepare you for the 'magic roundabout' located in Swindon. It's a set of 5 mini roundabouts on one large roundabout. Once we navigated that we went for a walk around the ground. We found a sports complex behind one of the stands had a game going on, so we stood and watched for a while. As we were dressed in our usual black and white colours a few locals asked if we fancied a game of 5-a-side with them. It was all good friendly stuff, as it should be.

The match itself saw David Kelly give Newcastle a one goal lead at halftime, but two goals inside the opening ten minutes of the second half put the hosts in front. Even the introduction of Andy Cole, making his debut, couldn't salvage anything.

30/11/94 – Maine Road

This game was the first away game I'd driven to, and what made it worse was I was by myself. I never had such a thing as a sat-nav or mobile phone so I had to trust my map reading skills and hope for the best. The only reason I went to this game was because my brother was staying in Manchester, and had a spare ticket if I wanted it. I arrived in decent time, and found where I was to meet up for my ticket.

Newcastle had quite a large following for this game, and were housed in the half built stand that ran along the side of the pitch. Mike Jeffery scored for us, but the scores were levelled in the second half. I said my goodbyes and walked back to where I'd left my car and drove home. It was quite brave of me, or stupid, to be walking alone around the back streets of Moss side after dark. Incidentally, when Mike Jeffery was sold to Rotherham that summer, my good friend Steve bought his house.

10

21/1/95 – Hillsborough

Since the disaster that tragically happened at this stadium in 1989, I had looked forward to visiting this place as a mark of respect. I recall sitting in my bedroom with Steve listening to the events unfold on the radio and not realizing at the time the huge affect this would have on future football matches. Fittingly, I went to this game with Steve, and also with my brother. It was absolutely pouring down with rain and we were soaked by the time the game kicked off. The game was a 0-0 draw and the only points of interest was that Newcastle were wearing a one-off green third strip. There was a debut for Keith Gillespie as a second half sub, and former toon player Chris Waddle was in the Sheffield starting eleven.

22/8/95 – Burnden Park

The start of the following season saw a familiar couple of faces jump in my car for an away trip to newly-promoted Bolton Wanderers. They were Steve and Bryan. We stood behind the goal towards the left as on the right part of the terrace was a supermarket.

This was my first glimpse of a French winger called David Ginola, and I must say, his cross for Les Ferdinand's header was excellent. Rob Lee scored a header in front of us, and then Ferdinand went on a powerful run before smashing the ball home for his second to send us all wild, winning 3-1.

8/4/96 – Ewood Park

Newcastle were at the top of the table but had been caught by Manchester United in the run in. They had collected only 7 points out of a possible 21 before this game on Easter Monday. Again, it was the usual three stooges of Steve, Bryan and I who headed down the motorway, to see Newcastle take on the current champions Blackburn, with Alan Shearer in their line-up. The game itself was a tight affair but when David Batty scored against his former club with only 15 minutes to go, the

11

atmosphere in the away end was amazing. However, another Geordie, Graham Fenton scored in the 86th and 89th minute to stun the travelling fans.

26/8/97 – Victoria Park

There was an offer in one of the daily newspapers, where if you collected so many tokens you could attend certain football matches for free. The game between Hartlepool United and Tranmere Rovers in the Coca-Cola Cup was one. I took my son Scott to give him a taste of live football, however with a crowd of less than 2,000 this was nothing like he had previously seen on TV. The game ended with Hartlepool winning 2-1 but they went out on aggregate. Playing for Hartlepool was an old school friend of mine called Micky Barron, and the scorer for Tranmere that day was ex-Newcastle legend Liam O'Brien.

8/11/97 – Highfield Road

A trip to Coventry was organized for a few of us, and this match is one which will stand out in a few people's memories. With only four minutes on the clock Shay Given caught the ball, and then looked to the kick it up field from off the ground. However, Dion Dublin was behind him and slotted the ball into the empty net. The joke of the day was 'Shay Given is the only Irishman not to know where Dublin was'. Newcastle scored through John Barnes before Dublin got his second. Robert Lee hit a 30 yard screamer into the top corner to earn the toon a point. Newcastle wore their usual black and white striped shirts but with white socks and white shorts.

18/11/97 – Pride Park

Derby County had just opened their new stadium at the start of the season, and although I never visited The Baseball Ground, Steve and I decided a midweek trip in the cup would be ideal.

The ground was quite impressive, built near an industrial estate which is where I parked.

Derby County had never been beaten at their new stadium in a competitive match until Jon Dahl Tomasson scored to send Newcastle through 1-0.

Our happiness was short lived, as when we got back to the car a lovely £30 parking ticket was waiting for us. This made the journey a little more expensive than was needed.

5/4/98 – Old Trafford

The FA Cup semi final against Sheffield United was to be my first visit to Old Trafford. The usual three of us, Steve, Bryan and I booked onto a supporters coach to take us to this game. We got there fairly early and found a bar which was showing the other semi final between Arsenal and Wolves. Bryan and I had tickets for the front row, right on the half way line while Steve was sitting in the upper tier of the huge North Stand. The only goal of the game came from Alan Shearer on the hour mark which had the whole stand shaking with the celebrations of the Geordie faithful. When I got home on the Sunday night, I headed straight to Grange Villa club to continue celebrating. Everyone was telling me that the TV cameras had zoomed in on the back of my shirt as I was standing with both arms aloft waving at my mate in the upper tier. They knew it was me as the name on the back of the shirt was not one of the heroes out on the pitch, but simply 'PODGE', number 5.

22/8/98 – Deepdale

This trip to Preston came about when Steve and I were having a weekend away staying in Blackpool. As Blackpool were playing away, a quick check of the fixture list showed that Preston were at home against Stoke City in Division Two. It's only about a 30 minute drive along the M55 so we headed there. We both were wearing our black & white Newcastle tops so we knew we were not going to stand in the away section, as Stoke wear red &

white. We found a bar right behind the stand known locally as the 'town end'. We were made to feel very welcome by the locals and had a great bit of football chat with them. We stood behind the goal with a few of the locals in the newly renamed 'toon end' and watched a decent game that the away side won 4-3.

20/4/99 – St Andrews
I was working away in Birmingham, and instead of staying in a hotel room all night I decided on a trip to see Birmingham play QPR in Division One on a Tuesday night. I was on my own so decided to sit behind the goal near the away fans to feel a bit of the atmosphere. Sadly, the atmosphere was non-existent and the only song I heard made me chuckle…
'Cockney scum, get out of the Brum'
The game was as poor as the chant, and only one goal saw the Brummies take all three points.

24/4/99 – Brunton Park
A friend of mine from the Chester Boys side Craig Liddle was playing for Darlington, and on this Saturday they were away to Carlisle in Division Three. That morning, I asked Steve if he fancied a trip to see it. He agreed, so we headed across the country and decided to sit with the away fans.
The game itself was a six goal thriller and 'Lidds' scored and celebrated in front of us. It was a point each for Carlisle in their successful bid to avoid the drop and for Darlington in their failed quest for promotion. I think most of the 4,000 crowd went home content.
We headed home on the A69 passing the delights of Hexham and Hayden Bridge along the way, stopping off for a piss-stop half way home.

2/11/99 – Feethams

Once again Steve and I thought another trip down the motorway to see Darlington play at home would be a good idea. We chose a Tuesday night game against Leyton Orient. We stood in the accurately named Shed End, with just over 4,500 fans in attendance. Darlo had ex-Sunderland player Marco Gabbiadini playing for them and I must say when he scored twice I could not bring myself to celebrate, even though the hardy home fans were jubilantly jumping around us.

CHAPTER 3

The Millennium Onwards

19/3/00 – Goodison Park

The game away at Everton was selected live for Sky TV and moved to the Sunday. Gary Lee said he would drive, so Steve and I agreed to join him on the trip. I had recently changed jobs and was now working at Asda Gateshead, and two lads from there came along as well, Parker and Wigs.

When we got near the ground we stopped at traffic lights and noticed the familiar face of Mark Hughes in the car opposite. He was playing for Everton that day so we duly gave him some stick before he sped away when the lights went green. The game itself came alive late in the second half when Aaron Hughes scored for Newcastle then Kieron Dyer scored a great solo effort to send us all home happy.

On the way back, we stopped at Kirby Stephens for a pint, and one of the local gentlemen took a fancy for Gary and asked if he could give him his number. Gary politely told him to f*ck off and went and sat in the car while we finished our beers. We managed to visit the Chinese takeaway called Panda Express. Wigs asked for a Panda House Special curry, but said he would prefer chicken and beef instead of Panda. The fella who was serving us didn't have a clue; either that or the Geordie accent was completely bemusing him. As it was rather late, Gary set off and allowed us to carry on munching on our food in his car. When Wigs had had enough of his Panda-less curry he decided to throw it out of the car window. Now, I don't think he calculated the wind factor of doing 70mph, as half of it flew back into his face and the other half ended down the side of Gary's white Mondeo.

11/11/00 – Filbert Street

Asda Gateshead had a number of other Newcastle fans working there, and this is where the group of attendees started to alter from the usual. One of our ex-workmates Tony Elliott had moved to Leicester earlier that year so we decided to go to the game, stay over and have a night out with him. I drove, and Steve, Kenny and Sheeran came as well. The car and the bags were dropped off at the hotel, and it was straight to the pub.

We entered the ground through what looked like someone's front door and stood along the side of the pitch. Sheeran was a young lad who worked for me and got so pissed on the way that he could hardly stand, never mind see the game. He just kept repeating 'Filbat Street' whenever asked where we were playing.

The home side opened the scoring with a great free kick before Gary Speed equalized for Newcastle. That's pretty much all I can remember as well, as I too had a couple of drinks pass my lips.

We returned to the digs to get changed and headed out meeting up with Tony in the main drinking area of Leicester. Towards the end of the night Kenny was trying his best to pull a local lass, he wasn't bothered how old or how big. Eventually, he disappeared into the night. No-one had mobile phones then so we hoped to see him soon. In the early hours, we said our goodbyes to Tony and headed for the hotel. I was rooming with Steve, and Sheeran was in with the missing-in-action Kenny. Sheeran was so drunk Steve and I had to put him to bed. We stripped him to his boxers and tucked him in. When I say 'tucked him in', what I meant was, we emptied the contents of the free coffee sachets, sugar, teabags, and milk cartons over his head while he slept. We even stuck little bars of soap on his cheeks before hitting the sack ourselves.

The following morning around 8am, we were awoken by the sound of Kenny in the corridor outside our door. He had been to an all night bar with some lesbian. He didn't score after all, but his wallet was pretty empty. We set off on the Sunday morning with Kenny telling us he had to go straight to work as he was on the rota for a shift starting at 5pm. He made it to work in time but in such a mess that he ended up in a disciplinary for the sackable offence of attending work drunk. He asked me to be his representative in the hearing, and I assured the panel that he was tired and not drunk. He kept his job…..just.

17/1/01 – Villa Park

Newcastle had drawn at home in the FA Cup third round which meant a replay against Aston Villa. I packed the car with four lads and headed to the 'second city' on a cold Wednesday night. The team had a few injuries and it showed. We had Marcelino at the back, and Cordone came off the bench in the second half. Villa had David James in goal, Southgate at the back, Paul Merson playing in midfield and Dion Dublin up front. The game was awful to watch. Villa scored the only goal of the game just after half time. The ball hit Darius Vassell and trickled past Harper into the net. After the game, we went to a pub to let the traffic ease before setting off on the trip home. The other lads in the car were getting dropped off at their homes which meant I had to pass the Chester le Street junction on the A1, and keep going north to Blaydon. It was approx 2am and I'm flooring it past the Metrocentre when suddenly blue lights appear behind me. The officer asks me to get into the back of his car, I hand over my license and the conversation goes like this,

Police – There are three lads in the back without seat belts on.

Me – They are all over 18 so it's not my responsibility.

Police – No, but driving at 90 mph is your responsibility, isn't it?

I never answered and thought bollocks, stop trying to be clever, he's going to do me here.

Police – Why are you travelling north in the early hours with a car full of lads, when your address is Chester le Street?

Me – I've been to the Newcastle match at Aston Villa and I'm dropping the lads off who all live in Newcastle.

Police – Shit game was it?

Me – Yes, we could have still been playing now, and still wouldn't have scored.

Police – Well, you're lucky I'm a Newcastle fan so get yourself away, drop the lads off, and slow down.
Me – Yes sir, thank you sir!!

31/3/01 – Valley Parade

This trip goes down in folklore as being one of the greatest trips to an away ground. Nine of us decide we want to go to the Bradford game so I look for cheap mini bus hire. Whilst searching I see an advert for a limousine hire company, and give them a call. How much to hire a limo for to go to Bradford and back for a match? After a bit of pause the bloke says £360. My quick maths work it out at £40 a man, yes that will do, we'll have it. On the morning of the game, the limo turns up and the driver looks like Dolph Lundgren. He's about 6ft 5, built like a tank. He says, the boss has asked me to take this trip as he doesn't want his limo smashed up, he's put some beers in the back for you, and after the game I'll treat you all to a MacDonald's if there's no damage!! Result.

There was me, Steve, Stansfield, Kenny, Iain, Parker, Stu, Wigs and Sheeran all merrily drinking away when Wigs, who was wearing this huge St Patrick's Day Guinness hat, was frantically trying to lower the window he was sitting next to. It wasn't working, so he was now becoming white as a sheet. He then grabbed the hat off his head and proceeded to throw up into the hat. Last night's supper and this morning's beer was now outside instead of in. We needed a piss-stop so the driver pulled over onto the hard shoulder, where the hat, and its contents, was discarded. The sight of nine blokes, all dressed in black and white shirts, pissing into the trees alongside a limo must have been quite a sight for the passing traffic. We got to Bradford and Dolph parked the limo near a pub full of Geordies. We asked if we should meet back here after the game, which was agreed but not before he came with us to the bar. It was so full it was taking ages to get served. The man-mountain decided he would make his way to the front. He did this without any trouble and ordered for us. We all stood outside as it was a nice day and witnessed

19

something funny, but not funny, at the same time. A local, wearing his full Asian dress, crossed the road in front of us. A car slammed on the brakes, but it was too late. What looked like a huge white sheet flew up into the air and landed on the bonnet. It looked as though he had just driven through someone's washing line. This looked serious, but in a matter of five seconds, the lad just stood up and walked away as if nothing had happened.

As we walked to the ground we passed a sex-shop, so obviously nine blokes just had to pay it a visit. Among all of the dirty videos, someone found one called 'The Shit Gang 4', to which Parker replied 'I haven't seen the first three yet!!'

Stansfield and I spotted the stadium from where we were and headed in that direction. We were heading towards a railway line with no access to allow us to cross but that didn't stop us from trying. As we approached, there was an announcement from a loud speaker coming from a parked up police van. He said something like 'Don't you dare go over there or you will be arrested. Walk back this way and around the car-park'. We did exactly as he said. The match itself was a bit of a blur, but Bradford went two up within the first ten minutes. Carl Cort and a second half equalizer from Clarence Acuna rescued a point for Newcastle.

What a day, what a way to travel to an away game.

21/4/01 – Stadium of Light

My first visit to Sunderland's pathetically named stadium came in Newcastle's second visit. The order of the day was for me to get to St. James' Park for approximately 3pm in order to climb on board a free bus across to the dark-side. There were 37 (I counted them…) double-decker buses supplied by Newcastle to ship our hoards of fans safely to the game. We arrived under heavy police presence over an hour before the 5.15pm kick-off and marched straight in. The good thing was that the bars were open and serving alcohol.

The game itself was a typical derby game with the odd late tackle going in. The mackems went in front when the ball went through the legs of Shay Given. Their celebrations didn't last long as Andy O'Brien etched his name into a Geordie-song folklore hero when he scored in front of the Newcastle fans. Liam O'Brien, Andy O'Brien, any, any, any O'Brien.

After the final whistle we were kept in the stadium for 25 minutes before being shuffled back onto the buses to make our way back to St James'. I arrived into Newcastle around 8.30pm, and then had to get home from there. I managed to spend the last few hours of the day in the Villa club, before retiring drunkenly to bed.

13/10/01 – Reebok Stadium

The newly opened Reebok Stadium was built near a retail park which included an Asda store. As we worked for Asda, I asked our store manager to contact his counterpart at the Horwich store to see if we could park my car there when we went. He agreed so we set the off for there. There were five of the 'limo nine' in the car and on entering the stadium Kenny asked one of the stewards if it was ok for him to wear his Adidas trainers in the Reebok stadium. The steward obviously didn't understand the joke, and politely said he would be ok.

Newcastle opened the scoring through Nobby Solano, before the big tuning point of the game. On the hour mark Jussi Jaaskelainen, the Bolton keeper was correctly sent off for hand ball outside the box, and with no sub keeper on the bench, it was a case of how many we would get. Three more goals were scored by Robert, Shearer and Bellamy to send us all home happy.

30/1/02 – White Hart Lane

During our summer holiday, the wife and I made friends with a Tottenham Hotspur fan called Steve, and his girlfriend Sara, who lived just south of London in West Sussex. He said when Newcastle played Spurs, we could stay at his house and we could travel to the game together. I drove to West Sussex on the Wednesday morning with my wife Jackie and son Scott, who would be spending time with Sara, and my other mate Steve. Cockney Steve then escorted us to his beloved team's ground via train and tube. Cockney Steve had his ticket behind the goal, next to the away fans so we could meet up easily after the game. When Spurs scored just in front of Cockney Steve, I could see him waving frantically at us in celebration. I think I gave him a two-fingered wave back. In the second half, Acuna equalized for Newcastle, and then Shearer put us in front two minutes later. Craig Bellamy wrapped up the points for the toon and it was now me who was waving frantically at Cockney Steve. I don't think he saw me, though!! We stayed at Cockney Steve's that night, setting off in the morning after a hearty breakfast was served for us. Cheers Steve.

11/5/02 – St Mary's Stadium

Cockney Steve came up trumps again with the offer of accommodation for this long drive to the south coast. My other mate Steve came along, as did Sheeran. I got Cockney Steve a ticket in the away end with us. It was the last day of the season and Southampton's greatest ever player Matt Le Tissier was on the bench for his last competitive game before retiring. The Newcastle players were already thinking about their summer holidays and it showed. Shearer scored against his former club, but we were already two down by then. Kieron Dyer was then halved by Southampton's Moroccan player El Khalej, who was duly sent off. His World Cup dreams seemingly over when he was stretchered off. The Saints scored again in the last minute, but there was no farewell appearance of Le Tissier, apart from the usual end of season lap of honor.

11/1/03 – Upton Park

These trips down south were becoming quite regular, and once again Cockney Steve's house was the location of our weekend stay. In the car for this journey were Jackie, Gavin and his girlfriend Louise. We had all holidayed in Cyprus during the summer so it was a bit of a get together for all six of us. Again, it was only the lads going to the match, and again Cockney Steve was coming in the toon away end. Most of the talk before the game was that Lee Bowyer had signed for West Ham after his contract at Leeds had expired. A selection of the hammers fans were demonstrating outside the ground, questioning his attitude towards racism after his court appearances for an assault charge.

Before the game, the three of us headed into London on the train, and went into a pub full of West Ham fans near the ground. The atmosphere was good and we were chatting to a few groups of local fans. Newcastle opened the scoring through Craig Bellamy but West Ham went in a goal up at half time. The points were shared in the second half when Jermaine Jenas hit a rocket of a shot into the roof of the net. After the game we decided to go back to the same pub to let the crowds disperse, but the atmosphere had notably changed. They didn't seem to be happy to see black & white shirts in here now. We quickly finished our pints before heading off back to the tube, with our colours zipped away under our coats.

11/5/03 – The Hawthorns

This was the last day of the season, so all the usual lads wanted to go to see Newcastle play already relegated West Bromwich Albion. However, for some reason tickets were hard to come by and there was only me who managed to get one. I booked onto a supporter's bus and sat all alone on the way there. We stopped off at a pre-arranged pub for a few beers before heading to the ground. Newcastle scored first before conceding two, then securing a point with a well taken free kick from Hugo Viana. You could tell this was a bit of a non-event as the referee didn't once show a yellow or red card, as most players didn't want to be injured on the beach. This result meant we finished third in the Premiership and qualified for next season's Champions League again.

26/12/03 – Walkers Stadium

Leicester City had opened their new stadium at the start of the previous season so a Boxing Day trip seemed ideal. I decided to drive and Gareth Bell came along for the trip. The game was apparently Leicester's 4,000th league game and to celebrate, they charged £4 for a programme instead of £2.50. In the home team's line-up was Sir Les Ferdinand, who was warmly greeted with applause from the travelling fans. It was another poor show from Newcastle on the pitch and inevitably Leicester took the lead. However, they didn't extend their lead when chance after chance went begging, and paid the price in the 90th minute when Newcastle's substitute Darren Ambrose headed in and sent the lads wild.

10/1/04 – Reynolds Arena

Darlington had also moved into their new stadium, and my mate Craig invited me and Scott along to watch him in their Division Three game with Hull City. Free match tickets and a pass into the player's lounge are always well received. Hull City brought a large following in their promotion season and a crowd of just under 7,000 saw the visitors win 1-0. We waited in the player's area after the game and Craig came in shaking everyone's hand, saying hello, and signing autographs. He walked across to us, opened his kitbag and gave Scott his match-worn away shirt from their last game. Scott was completely made up, especially with all the envious eyes of the other kids around us gazing in his direction.

3/2/04 – Riverside Stadium

Middlesbrough were playing in the semi-final of The Carling Cup against Arsenal and a mate from work asked me if I fancied it. I only said yes as I had not been to their new ground. I asked another mate Paul Welsh, a 'Boro season ticket holder, if I could grab a lift and it was agreed. Middlesbrough had won the first leg at Highbury 1-0 so the locals were full of expectation of a

Wembley final day out. We sat behind the goal with the travelling Cockneys to our left. Martin Keown was sent off near the end of the goal-less first half. Bolo Zenden scored for the hosts before Arsenal equalized. However, the home support went mad when they scored again to win 2-1 on the night. In the car on the way home, I was asked if I would want tickets for the final but I kindly refused the offer.

29/2/04 – Fratton Park

Once again my Cockney mate Steve came up trumps with the offer of a weekend at his place, which coincided with a trip to the south coast to see Newcastle play at Portsmouth. We headed to Steve's early on the Saturday to enjoy a night out, before the taking in the match on the Sunday. Another few beers on the evening before the long drive home on Monday.

In the Pompey starting eleven were ex-Newcastle player Shaka Hislop and current Newcastle player Lomana Lua Lua, who was on loan. Why any club would allow their own player to play against them while on loan is ludicrous. Fratton Park's four stands only had three roofs and yes the away fans were stood in the one without. It was a cold day but thankfully it was dry. Things warmed up when Craig Bellamy scored in front of the away fans to give us a half time lead. The interval saw a former Pompey and Toon player welcomed onto the pitch, none other than Mick Quinn. He was applauded by all. With 89 minutes on the clock, you guessed it, Lua Lua equalized for the home team before celebrating with his usual string of back flips. Typical Newcastle!!

23/1/05 – Highbury

In all my years of going to football matches, I can honestly say that I have never been as drunk at a match as I was at this one. Once again my Gunners-hating Spurs mate Steve came along not to support Newcastle but to hate everything Arsenal. The wife and I arranging another weekend down south in order for me to take in this Sunday afternoon live TV match. We travelled into London early on the morning, arriving near the ground a few hours before kick-off. Steve wore his Tottenham shirt under his coat as we walked into a bar full of Red & White shirts and scarves. Fortunately for him I spotted his collar with the words 'SPURS' on it, sticking out over the top of his jacket. With that we sampled the beer and got chatting to some locals. Steve pretended to be a Leyton Orient fan so as not get his head kicked in. We headed into the ground found our seats behind the goal near the corner flag. Just before the start I saw my two brother-in-laws, Ray and Kevin, standing in the small section of travelling fans along the side of the pitch, and wanted to see them. However, as I mentioned earlier, the beer had taken over and I attempted to walk across the corner of the pitch towards them. I was then forcefully pushed back into my section with the threat of being ejected from the ground by the stewards. The major talking point before the game was that Craig Bellamy had feigned injury and wouldn't play. Newcastle lost 1-0 thanks to a goal from Dennis Bergkamp but it could have been lots more if it wasn't for Shay Given in the Newcastle goal. I only know this as I watched the game three days later on video, borrowed from Ray who had taped it off Sky TV.

2/2/05 – City of Manchester Stadium

If anyone has ever met a lad called Paul Piggford who used to play for Grange Villa, you will know what a crazy fella he is. He is a Sunderland fan, as well as a Glasgow Rangers fan, but also drives a minibus. He agreed to taxi eight Geordies to the new stadium belonging to Manchester City, who were now managed by Kevin Keegan. He refused a ticket for the match preferring to fall asleep in the bus. Along came a few of the lads including Wigs, Mick Day, and my son Scott for this Wednesday evening fixture. Alan Shearer opened the scoring at the opposite end to the away fans after only 9 minutes. Robbie Fowler equalized from the spot early in the second half and the game ended without further goals.

After the game, we headed back to the bus and made our way to a MacDonald's drive-thru. Paul was relaying every order that was shouted to him from the back of the bus in a strange Jamaican voice to confuse the person taking the order through the intercom system. Incredibly, every order was spot on, and we quickly tucked these away and headed home.

19/11/05 – Stamford Bridge

I took Scott to see Newcastle play Chelsea, and Cockney Steve came along as well. We were staying at his place again so it was only right the lads went to the match while the ladies went shopping. We headed for a pub near the ground which was packed with locals and not many away fans. Sensibly I sent my cockney mate to the bar so not to arouse any suspicions. However, Scotts Newcastle shirt was visible through his unfastened coat and a Chelsea fan said to him *'don't look so facking worried, mate. You'll be awight in ere'*. Our hosts were charging £45 for the privilege of watching this match. Although Newcastle were level at half time, second half goals from Joe Cole, Hernan Crespo and Damien Duff saw Chelsea run out comfortable winners in a fairly one sided game.

20/9/06 – Anfield

There was a mini bus organized for this game as a few lads wanted to go. We found this pub full of Liverpool fans to enjoy a few beers before the game. There was a huge screen showing a re-run of the Champions League final against AC Milan when Liverpool recovered from three goals down to win on penalties. The cheers from the locals when each goal went in was a bit strange but understandable.

Liverpool had Craig Bellamy in the starting line-up, and he got plenty of abuse from the away following every time the ball went near him. They took the lead in the first half when Dirk Kuyt scored from close range. This game will always be remembered though for Liverpool's second goal. Xabi Alonso collected the ball in his own half before booting it towards The Kop End goal. As it was in the air, the back peddling Steve Harper slipped and the ball went in over his head. Cue the wild celebrations from the Scousers.

26/7/08 – Keepmoat Stadium

Newcastle were playing a friendly against Doncaster Rovers in their new stadium so Bish and Sima were easily persuaded to come for a day out. I contacted the manager of the nearby Asda and requested a parking space, to which he agreed. The weather was fantastic; glorious sunshine scorching us all. Newcastle gave a debut to Sebastian Bassong, a young French lad who was on trial. However, no one in the away section knew anything about him, not even his name. He played quite well, so much that the crowd gave him his own song. It went something like this. 'Forty, Forty-six. Forty, Forty-six'. At half-time Shola Ameobi's younger brother Tomi, came on for Doncaster. The game looked to be heading for a nil-nil draw until the hosts scored with three minutes remaining.

26/8/08 – Ricoh Arena

I had entered a competition on the radio and won the use of a hire car for a few days, so thought it would be a good idea to rack up its mileage with a trip to Coventry's new stadium. Bish and Wigs came along for this Tuesday night out in the Midlands. Newcastle had been drawn away in the Carling Cup and the game was going out live on Sky. Newcastle raced into a two-goal lead thanks to Charles N'Zogbia and James Milner before the hosts pulled one back on the stroke of half time. The game was all but over when in the 93rd minute Coventry got a throw-in near the corner flag. What followed was one of the longest throws I've ever seen. It landed on the head of a fellow home player and the ball was steered home. That meant extra-time. Fortunately for us, Michael Owen scored and we went through

28

3-2. We knew this was going to mean a late night so we found a fish & chip shop for our suppers before heading off.

26/12/08 – JJB Stadium

This was another Boxing Day trip, this time to Wigan with Mick Day, Wigs and Scott. Hardly anything on the roads meant an easy drive down; and found the fairly deserted retail park near the ground. Good stuff. Wigan went ahead when Ryan Taylor hit a free kick, scoring for the third consecutive game against Newcastle. They went two up when the ref gave a penalty for a tussle between Bassong on Emile Heskey. This started well outside the area. Even the linesman was flagging for a free kick but Heskey stayed on his feet until inside the area then fell over. To make matters worse there was a red card for Bassong. Newcastle pulled one back when Danny Guthrie scored from the spot with two minutes remaining. Full time whistle went and we trundled off back to the car.

To complete an awful trip, a parking ticket, on Boxing Day? Merry fucking Christmas!!

14/3/09 – KC Stadium

Mick Day arranged this trip and offered to drive, with the added bonus of a Friday night out in York. His mate would allow us to crash at his place and we would go to the game from York to Hull on the Saturday morning. Mick, his mate Garry, me, Scott, Stansfield and Bish went mental on the night out in York, drinking well into the early hours. The following morning brought the news that we were getting the train from York to Hull. No one mentioned that!! I obviously had to pay for Scott, as he doesn't have cash. He just uses the bank of Mam and Dad. The game itself was as bad as my hangover. Chris Hughton was in temporary charge after the Joe Kinnear fiasco. Hull went in front but Steven Taylor equalized in front of the away fans, and that's as good as it got. The train ride back to York and the journey back home in Mick's car was a rather quiet one.

11/4/09 – *Britannia Stadium*

Newcastle's next away game had Alan Shearer in the hot seat, desperately trying to keep the team away from the relegation trap door. The car was filled with the usual suspects but also included Mick's son Daniel. This was a 5.30pm kick off which would mean another late return. The pre match warm up saw some of the Toon players having shooting practice in the goal in front of us. Now, we were in the front row of the middle section, and an Andy Carroll shot hit me full in the chest. I'd just seen it coming a split-second beforehand and avoided an embarrassing event.

Newcastle went behind but with time running out, substitute Andy Carroll headed home to salvage a point in this must-win game.

CHAPTER 4

The Championship Season & Beyond

22/8/09 – Selhurst Park
My cockney mate Steve had moved house and now lived in Croydon. This was ideal for when Newcastle, who had just been relegated, were playing at Crystal Palace in the Championship. I drove to Steve's on the Friday afternoon, staying for the weekend as usual, with Jackie and Scott. On the morning of the game, me, Scott and Cockney Steve caught the local bus and a twenty minute ride dropped us off right near the ground.

Newcastle had started the season well so there was once again a sold-out away section. Newcastle were wearing their awful yellow striped shirts, and two minutes into the game Kevin Nolan had put us in front. Ryan Taylor doubled the lead and that's how the game ended.

On the way home, we again jumped on the local bus service, and sat on the seats near the front. The bus was full due to the match. A few stops along the way two elderly ladies got on and no-one battered an eyelid. They were stood trying to grab hold of the straps as the bus pulled away. Without a thought I immediately stood up and offered the ladies our seats. When they sat down, one of them remarked to us 'you're not from round here are you?' I replied by saying 'is it my Geordie accent that gave me away?' to which she amazed me by saying 'no, it's because you gave us your seat. No-one ever does that here.'

16/9/09 – Bloomfield Road
The game every toon fan wanted to go to since relegation was Blackpool away. Typically, the fixture list gave us this on a Wednesday night. So, Wigs agreed to drive and along came Parker, Mick Day and Jonny Mac. We got to the ground fairly early and noticed that one of the gates was open, so in we walked. Parker stepped over the advertising boards and walked

onto the pitch before someone in a suit shouted at us and told us to get out. We calmed the bloke down and asked if we could get a photo in the dugout. After a little persuasion, he agreed as long as we left immediately. This is where my obsession of getting a dugout photo stemmed from.

We headed for the bars along Blackpool's Golden Mile, and even got interviewed by the local TV news reporters. When our mug-shots appeared on the 6 o'clock news the roar in the bar was as deafening as if we were celebrating a goal.

Blackpool's redeveloped ground was taking shape, however the stand behind one goal (The Jimmy Armfield Stand) was still closed, and the away fans were housed along the side of the pitch in temporary seating, with no roof. That's the reason for a crowd of less than 10,000.

Newcastle strangely wore their blue and black third kit for this game, when there would have been definitely no clash of colours between tangerine and black and white. Andy Carroll opened the scoring for the toon with a header but the hosts equalized before half time. A poor performance resulted in another Blackpool goal in the second half, and Newcastle lost their unbeaten record from the start of the season.

22/9/09 – London Road

Newcastle were drawn away to Peterborough in The Carling Cup and as it was a Tuesday night game, a day off work was needed. Along for the ride came Bish, Mick Day and his son Daniel. We arrived in fairly good time, a couple of hours before kickoff. We parked up and walked around the ground. We spotted a steward stood near a big gate which led into the corner of the ground. I asked him if we could get a photo in the dugout, which after some persuasion using Daniel's birthday as an excuse, he agreed and escorted us along the side of the pitch for a photo. Once we had the photo taken the steward was desperately trying to get us to leave, but I had spotted the Peterborough Chairman Barry Fry, being interviewed by a local news reporter. The steward was shitting himself as I walked up to him to ask for a photo.

Barry Fry was a great sport and walked us onto the pitch for the photo. I remarked that the sign says 'Keep off the grass', to which he replied 'It's my grass!'.

Newcastle played a lot of the reserves, fringe players, youth team, whatever you want to call them, and they were awful. Four players were making their debut and it showed. This game did nothing to help their chances of selection in a league game. The toon were 2-0 down at half-time and early in the second half, Danny Guthrie was sent off. You could have blown the whistle for full time right then as Newcastle whimpered out of this competition.

20/10/09 – Glanford Park

Another Tuesday night game saw Newcastle play away to Scunthorpe in the league. This was Newcastle's first ever visit to this ground. Bish and Mick Day came along again but replacing Mick's son in the car was Jonny Mac.

We parked the car in the stadium car park for only £3, and headed in search of a dug out photo. This seemed to be quite easy and we headed in and sat in what looked like a bus shelter. I couldn't help myself being this close, so I got a photo stood on the pitch, much to the annoyance of the steward.

The game was another poor show from Newcastle. Goal-less at half-time, we fell behind, equalized, fell behind again, full time whistle. After the game we decided to let the traffic die down, so headed for the Pizza Hut just opposite the stadium. When we got there and placed our orders, the fella serving us said there could be a delay as they have had an order for 25 pizzas. He then informed us it was for the Newcastle team bus... We all agreed it must have been Geremi who came for them after he got subbed off in the second half!!

27/2/10 – Vicarage Road

Newcastle were doing well in the Championship by now so my car was loaded with Bish, Jonny, Mick and his son Daniel for the trip to Watford. We arrived fairly early and attempted the dugout photo. The steward at the gate was having none of it, so I came up with some bullshit about doing it for The Bobby Robson Foundation Charity, saying we are doing it at every ground and so far we have not been turned down. He believed us and escorted us pitch-side. Just then the Newcastle team bus arrived and some of the players walked out to inspect the pitch. We grabbed hold of Danny Guthrie and got him to join us for the photo. We got our photo and headed for a nearby pub. Three lagers for the lads and two orange and sodas for me and Dan were ordered just as the bar erupted in Geordie songs.

The match saw the first airing of the 'Oh Coloccini' song just after he had given the toon an early lead. Andy Carroll doubled Newcastle's lead just after half time, before Watford pulled one back in stoppage time. We held on for the remaining few minutes for an excellent away win.

On loan defender Patrick Van Arnholt made his final appearance for Newcastle and was warmly applauded by the away following as we started to make our way out of the ground.

13/4/10 – Madejski Stadium

Newcastle's match away at Reading was on a Tuesday evening so an overnight stay was planned for this one. There were seven of us going so we took two cars. Ridley, his wife, Jonny and Gary went in one car, and Bish and Stansfield came in mine. We arrived at the hotel, dropped the bags off and set off for the ground and bars. We jumped in a taxi and told the driver to take us to the ground. The driver was called Safraz, and I told him there was 'an extra pound in it for him' if he put his foot down. He assured us we could get a pint near to the stadium. Safraz was wrong. We were told we could get a drink in the hotel attached to the stadium but this was for hotel residents only.

We decide to walk around the stadium and bumped into the Reading chairman, and the man the stadium is named after, Sir John Madejski. He duly stopped for photos and we headed for the area where the stewards had gathered for the pre-match briefing. I asked the question about a dug out photo and all seven of us were allowed in for a group shot. As we were coming out of the stadium, a local news reporter asked us for an interview which is to go out on local radio. As we were the biggest away following all season, we were looked upon as the division's big boys. A couple of us agreed to the interview which, in all honestly, I doubt they would use on air.

Kevin Nolan scored twice in the first half to give Newcastle, dressed in their yellow kit, a comfortable lead. Reading scored just after halftime thanks to a comical own goal, but Newcastle held on to take the points ensuring that only one more point was needed to take the title.

The jubilant group then enjoyed a pleasant night out in the bars of Reading before heading back to the hotel in the early hours.

19/4/10 – Home Park

Sky TV are great aren't they? This game was moved to a Monday night for live transmission. It also meant another hotel stay over. Mick Day had agreed to drive to this one but pulled out due to work commitments. So that left Jonny and me. Jonny doesn't drive, and the costs of train or flights were extortionate. The hotel had been booked and paid for, so it meant I would be driving my trusty MG for the 800 miles round trip. As there was a spare ticket going, my brother-in-law Ray jumped at the chance of coming along for the momentous occasion.

We set off early on the Monday morning, arriving around the 3 o'clock mark. Throughout the seven hour journey, we only had one cd, The Smiths Greatest Hits. We now know the lyrics to every track. The bags were dumped in the room and we headed off to find the bars. The weather was glorious so it was short sleeved Newcastle tops only. We found a bar which had just installed a huge 3D television, and the barman gave us the glasses to try out. It was quite a sight seeing a tennis ball heading straight for you while trying not to spill your beer.

After a few pints we headed for the ground. It was quite a walk through some parks to get to the stadium. We walked around the ground and asked for usual dugout photo. The Plymouth stewards were excellent with us, and walked us down to the pitch. As we were having our photo taken, the Newcastle players made their way onto the pitch, similar to what happened at Watford. This time I shouted of Joey Barton to come over. He came across and when he got to us I asked him to take our photo. He replied 'Are you taking the piss?' We then asked the steward to take a photo of Joey Barton taking our photo in the dugout. Without this photo I doubt anyone would believe this story. We got photos with Joey as well, and he kept calling Ray a bumble-bee as he was wearing the yellow strip. The same strip as he would be wearing in a couple of hour's time. We stepped onto the pitch for another photo, and this time the steward was politely telling us to stop taking advantage of his good nature.

We walked to the away end and sampled a couple of pints before the game started. Before kick off a few young Plymouth fans unfurled a banner in front of us which said 'Congratulations Newcastle, From The Green Army'. This was a nice touch considering their own team was headed for relegation. First half goals from Andy Carroll and Wayne Routledge at the opposite end of the ground meant the Geordie fans never stopped singing. When eventually the final whistle was blown, a number of fans attempted to get on the pitch, and were halted by around ten stewards. They could not stop the entire away end that then filtered down the terrace towards the pitch. The three of us joined the masses and celebrated with the players. We even headed for the dug outs and got another photo just because we could.

We made our way back to the hotel for a quick change of tops and headed for the bars. As it was a Monday night, it wasn't very busy. One bar was selling pints 2 for the price of 1. Ray bought two, and before he had managed a half, the lights went up, the music turned off, and the bouncers were ordering us to drink up.

We managed to drink up and found a night club. The place was jumping. We thought we would mingle with the locals, but everyone we spoke to had a Geordie accent. The club closed at 2am and all you could hear was Newcastle songs being sung at the top of Geordie voices. We headed for food then headed for the hotel. We didn't have breakfast included in the room price so Ray finished off last night's cold kebab including the garlic dip. We set off on the long trip home with The Smiths blasting out. Happy Days.

2/5/10 – Loftus Road

The last game of the Championship winning season was away at QPR. We booked the train for this Sunday game, with me, Stansfield, Jonny and Ridley heading south. The weather in Newcastle was hot so, once again, we only had short sleeved toon tops on. When we got to London, it was lashing down, and it was cold. We got to the ground but didn't bother with the dugout photo. We just wanted to be somewhere warm. Our seats were in the back row of the upper tier. It was freezing up there. The wind was blowing into our faces, and causing our soaked tops to cling to our bulky frames.

The game itself was much of a non-event. However, the fans were in full voice all afternoon. Ex-Toon player Peter Ramage was in the QPR side and was sent off just after half time. This man advantage allowed Newcastle to control the game and when Peter Lovenkrands lobbed the ball into the net in front of the away end, it was a deserved victory.

Once the usual players celebrating with the fans at the end of the season had finished, we headed for a bar till it was time for the train home. We went into the Walkabout pub where a live band was playing. We started off drinking sensibly but when Ridley returned from the bar with pints and shots, it started to get messy. We headed for Kings Cross via Shepherds Bush tube station where we got our photos taken with a couple of policemen. Like excited school kids we asked to wear their hats for the picture. They seemed to understand our high spirits and allowed us. As we were waiting for the last train out of Kings Cross, Stansfield shouted out 'KANT' for no reason whatsoever, and the local police officer here wasn't as nice as the ones we had earlier met. They informed him that they would let him on the train but throw him off at Peterborough. Now that is a strange punishment. Without any further incidents we headed north.

25/8/10 – Crown Ground

With Newcastle back in the Premier League, my first away trip wasn't very glamorous; it was a Wednesday night trip to Accrington Stanley in The Carling Cup. Bish, Stansfield, Ridley, Jonny and I managed to squeeze into my MG for the drive. We weren't far away from the ground and were struggling for a parking spot. A friendly lady offered me the chance of parking on her drive so as not to get a ticket, which the offer was quickly accepted.

Sky TV had once again taken our fixture with the hope of a giant-killing, and Accrington Stanley even milked it by charging £20 to stand in an uncovered end, as well as upping the price of a programme to £4.

There was to be no giant-killing though as a youthful Newcastle triumphed 3-2. After the game, our fully kitted out goal scorer Ryan Taylor, was chatting to some people near the exit so we grabbed him for a group photo. Stansfield asked him for his shirt for his nephew, who is called Taylor, but he declined saying he had promised it to one of the Stanley players. I asked for his shorts because my dog was called Taylor. He just shook his head. As my car was just outside the ground, we hung around near the team bus and when Alan Smith emerged from the dressing room areas, we grabbed him for a photo as well.

As we were driving home, my car started to slow down rapidly and all the lights were going dim, then all of a sudden it would come back to life and drive normally. Ridley also had an MG and he had never seen anything like it before. We were heading up the M6 when it started again; my thoughts were that it's going to be a long night if we break down. Thankfully we didn't, and made it home without too much hassle. We were flagged down by a police car that had blocked the road near Hexham to warn us of an accident, telling us to divert. Thankfully, the car didn't stall while we were stationary. The following day, the diagnosis from my son was a dodgy alternator, a new one required.

28/8/10 - Molineux
With my car out of action, the trip to Wolves three days later meant a coach trip. Me, Stansfield and Bish were the only survivors from Wednesday who went to this one. The usual routine of a few pints before the game, followed by a walk around the fairly impressive stadium took place. No dugout photo this time but I did get one next to the statue of Wolves legend Billy Wright.

Wolves took the lead before half time, but Andy Carroll headed home an equalizer for a deserved point.

30/10/10 – The John Smiths Stadium
Newcastle's game at home to Sunderland was moved to the Sunday, so there was a spare Saturday on the cards. I suggested to a few of the lads to pick a random game fairly close by, easily accessible by train, and have a day on the drink. Bish, Stansfield and Jonny were all up for it, so we decided on Huddersfield Town v Walsall in League One.

As Huddersfield were managed by ex-Newcastle player Lee Clark, I decided to send him an email telling him of our plans for 'derby-eve', and asked if we could meet up for a chat before the game. Amazingly, his secretary replied saying he would meet us if we got to the ground around 1pm. I didn't mention it to lads, but they started to get curious when I informed them we had to be at the ground two hours before kick-off. When we arrived I walked into reception and asked to speak to the secretary by name. She arrived and said, 'I'll take you round to see Lee Clark now.' The looks on the lads' faces were a picture. We walked into the Manager's office, and were greeted by Lee Clark. He introduced us to Terry McDermott, Paul Stephenson and Steve Black, all with Newcastle connections from the past, who were casually sitting round the office watching the horse racing on TV. We talked for about 15 minutes about all-things Newcastle, and predictions for the big game tomorrow. Eventually we had to say thank you, and allow them to get on with their work. We all got our photos to prove the story and headed out of the office. Instead of leaving, we headed for the dressing room area and sneaked into the away dressing room and nicked a couple of programmes and mars bars which were set out for the visiting players. From there, we walked out through the tunnel and grabbed the all important dug out photo. When security started give us strange looks we decided it was time to leave and head for the bar till kick-off.

Huddersfield had a player sent off early in the game but then took the lead. The rest of the game was all about defending and they hung on to take the points.

We returned to the station and sampled a few more beers before the journey home.

By the way, if you were wondering, the following day's result was Newcastle 5 Sunderland 1.

7/11/10 – Emirates Stadium

A trip to Arsenal's new stadium was always going to be a trip to remember. It was once again moved to a Sunday for Sky TV. Eugene agreed to drive if we agreed on a Saturday stay over with a night out in London on the evening before the game.

On the Saturday morning I received a phone call from LateRooms.com saying our room had been doubled booked, but he recommended a hotel in Finsbury Park. As we didn't have much choice I agreed. Bish and I jumped in Eugene's big posh BMW, and relaxed all the way there. When we arrived at the B&B an elderly Asian fella with no shoes on greeted us. I told him we had a triple room booked and he said we could have a twin on the top floor and a single in the basement. I said no, we want a triple room as booked.... safety in numbers. 'Follow me' he said and headed up the stairs. We looked at each other and followed. We got to the top of the stairs where he said 'you will need to move a bed from the adjacent room if you want a triple.' We agreed to move the bed but found it was just an old door on top of a frame, with a knackered mattress on top. Our room was the worst room I have ever stayed in. The three single beds were now cramped together; each bed had a different coloured sheet on it and a wafer thin pillow. The toilet and shower room was so small you couldn't wipe your arse without bumping your head on the wall. There was one curtain which didn't fully cover the window, and the dust in the room was playing havoc with Eugene's sinuses. We had to talk Eugene out of sleeping in his car overnight. The only positive was, as it was a cold November evening, the heating was on full blast. We got changed and headed to Camden Market for a good night out.

The following morning we headed to The Emirates for breakfast in a café nearby. There was no way we were going to see what breakfast would have been served at the hotel. We walked around the impressive stadium before meeting up with a cockney Newcastle fan Andy 'Panda', who we had a ticket for. Our seats were in the front row, right on the corner flag. Whenever we were noticed on live TV one of our phones would bleep with a message telling us we were spotted. The match was fairly even until Andy Carroll headed home at the far end of the stadium. The away fans slowly realized it had gone in and celebrated wildly. Newcastle held on to take a memorable three points, and we headed home after another great weekend.

8/1/11 – Broadhall Way

Newcastle were drawn away to Stevenage in the third round of the FA Cup, and as I didn't go to the game back in 1998 when the two sides met, I wasn't going to miss this one. Once again, the possibility of a cup upset meant that the game was selected for live television, this time by ESPN, with a Saturday evening kick-off of 5.30pm.

Me, Bish, Stansfield and Jonny decided we would go by train, stay in a hotel and have a night out in Stevenage. We were met at the hotel by Cockney Panda, his brother Warren, and Warren's young son. They were going to the game but obviously not the night out.

Typically, Newcastle crashed out against the League Two side. Two quick goals just after half time for the home team put them in control. Cheick Tiote was brought on as a sub but was soon red-carded for a crazy tackle. Joey Barton pulled one back in stoppage time, but with Newcastle throwing everyone forward Stevenage grabbed a third. The four of us jumped in a taxi, headed for the hotel to get changed, and then back out on the drink.

Stevenage was a bit of a strange night out but we eventually found a club which was 'the place to be'. As we were in there, one Stevenage player came strolling in wearing his full tracksuit. This meant we made a bee-line for him to give him some light-hearted abuse. Stansfield then acquired some pink glasses just like Kanye West wore, so we christened him John West.

2/2/11 – Craven Cottage

A Wednesday evening game in London can only mean one thing, another night out. This was another game selected by Sky TV. I managed to get cheap train tickets from Newcastle to Kings Cross with a return the following day. Six of us, me, Stanfield, Bish, Jonny, Gary Gilmour and my brother-in-law Paul met up with the two cockney Newcastle fans Warren and Panda for a day out in the smoke.

We were staying in a Travel Lodge with a bar nearby so that's where we went first. Well, that's where we stayed. It had a dart board and a replica of the World Cup. This was the prize. It was all going well until Stansfield threw a dart into Jonny's thigh…

Stansfield was on the sick at work so informed everyone not to take any photos of him and don't mention him being there on Facebook. Every photo opportunity saw him dive out of shot.

We eventually captured him a few times after the beer started flowing.

Outside the ground I got a photo next to the statue of Johnny Haynes as well as with two blokes who were dressed up like the Blues Brothers. It's a decent little ground with loads of character. When I watched the game back I saw myself three times on TV. On two of those occasions I was verbally abusing ex-Newcastle player Damien Duff. The little Irishman had the last laugh though as his goal saw Fulham win 1-0.

After the match finished and we were walking back to the hotel we noticed there was only one bar open. We headed there for a swift couple before closing time. We had somehow managed to acquire an exit sign from Craven Cottage so that came with us.

It was time to head for a kebab and we found this scruffy looking place and made our way in. Some local lass was shouting racial obscenities at the Asian fella behind the counter, but she got the message when we explained her errors and she soon left. We asked if we could use his toilet and he sent us down some stairs. We ended up in a strange basement with a large chest freezer. I opened it and decided, for no reason; I was having a frozen samosa and tucked it into my back pocket. After we all had been served we headed outside. To my amazement my samosa stealing had been trumped by Jonny's theft of a pair of flip-flops. Stansfield was tucking into his kebab when, for the first and only time in my life, I witnessed him drop his food all over the pavement. I was fucking howling as he booted it across the road. Paul saved the day with the offer of half of his pizza.

Back at the hotel we piled into Jonny's room with a couple of over-priced cans of lager bought from reception. Jonny then decided to entertain us by putting a bin over his head and then rubbed coffee into his face. He was now known as 'Jon Coffee'.

6/8/11 – The Don Valley Stadium
For my 40th birthday a group of 12 lads decided on two nights in Wakefield. We got smashed on the Friday night and decided to

go to a local game on the Saturday, and then get smashed again on the Saturday night.

Eight of the twelve lads decided on a short train trip to Sheffield, as Rotherham were playing their home games there while their new stadium was being built. It was the opening day of the season and the sun was scorching. Oxford United were the visitors for the League Two game. We had a group photo taken with Miller the Bear, Rotherham's mascot. It was a typical athletics venue with only one main stand. The standard of football on show was poor and the game ended 1-0 to the hosts. After the game I asked a steward for a dugout photo and he walked us around the pitch to the opposite side where they were located. In all honesty, we had just had a photo taken sitting on a park bench. Still, it broke the day up.

8/11/11 – Boundary Park

I was away on a course for work staying in Manchester on a Tuesday night when I noticed Oldham Athletic were playing Crewe in the Johnstones Paint Trophy. I was making my enquiries about travel arrangements of how to get there and back when one of the course tutors said she could drop me off as she lives nearby. She dropped me close enough to see the floodlights and I walked the rest of the way.

It was the first time in a number of years that I had attended a game where you could pay at the gate. I handed over the £10 fee and made my way to the main stand and sat near the Director's box. Considering there were just over 2000 in attendance, I could have sat anywhere. To my amazement, Lee Clark and Terry McDermott sat about four seats away to my left and as they sat down I said '*Alreet Clarkey?, Terry?*' in my strongest Geordie accent. They both acknowledged me, and I wondered if they actually recognized me from the Huddersfield Town meeting we had, or were they just being polite. I think it was the latter.

Oldham had Shefki Kuqi in their line-up after his release from Newcastle, as well as Manchester City manager Roberto

44

Mancini's son Andrea on the bench. The game itself was a decent affair and it was cult hero Kuqi who scored twice in a 3-1 win. After the game I had agreed to go to see my mate Jimmy D's girlfriend Lisa, who was singing in a bar in Manchester city centre. I stayed until around 1am forcing a couple of pints down.

10/12/11 – Carrow Road

A trip to Norwich by train was the order of the day, and this meant a very early start. Eugene, Stansfield, Bish, Jonny, Gary, Horspool and I got the 4.45am train from Newcastle to Peterborough. That was followed by two further trains eventually arriving around 10am just in time for breakfast. From there we found some pub and stayed there till near kick off.

Norwich were charging £45 for a ticket, the greedy bastards. The football on show from Newcastle wasn't great. Norwich took the lead but Demba Ba equalized just before half time. We were ripped off again during the interval. They were charging £3 for a pie…. and it was awful. 'Delia Smith, you're taking the piss.'

Norwich scored two more before the toon were down to ten men after Dan Gosling was sent off. There was a glimmer of hope when Ba got his second, but that was short-lived as Norwich got their fourth.

The three-train return journey became a four-train journey when we were informed of a cancellation. This meant we were in danger of missing our last train back to Newcastle from Peterborough. However, with only minutes to spare we caught it and arrived back just before midnight absolutely shattered, drunk and cold. That's what away days are all about.

28/1/12 – The AMEX Stadium

Newcastle were drawn away to Brighton, who were in the league below, in the FA Cup. Ridley drove to this one in a six-seater car, with the added bonus of a stay over. Jonny, Bish and I were joined by in the car by French Tony. A newly found friend of Jonny's, and as his name suggests, was originally from France and now living in the north-east. Newcastle was his adopted team in England. He is also 6ft 4in tall and seeing him squeeze into the back of the car for a seven hour journey was laughable. We pulled up at the hotel and dropped the car off. French Tony knew a few people in Brighton so he managed to get us a lift from the digs to the ground. The stadium is quite a distance from the city centre so you needed to get a train there.

The concourse for the away fans had the greatest sign above the kiosk I have ever seen. It simply said 'Beer and Pie'. Tremendous, what more could I want? The game itself was a typical Newcastle FA cup effort. A lackluster performance meaning we crashed out without a fight. We rolled over and lost 1-0 thanks to a Mike Williamson own goal. I had witnessed another giant-killing to add to the Stevenage debacle from last season.

The night out was decent though, but we made sure we stayed away from the gay scene. I even ended up on the DJ decks in some club. I don't know how or why I was there. The long old journey back home on the Sunday was quite painful.

6/4/12 – Liberty Stadium

A Good Friday trip to Wales was organized by Jonny with a stay over planned. There were 14 of us in total in the bus which included the usual suspects of Bish, Stansfield, Horspool and Paul. For some strange reason, Horspool had some James Perch face masks made so we could all wear them as some sort of cult fan club follower. We were dropped off at the stadium where we hit the bar. It was a pleasant day so we stood outside. Just as the Newcastle team bus appeared we all put on our 'Perchinio' masks, but I don't think he saw us.

Newcastle were in their orange away kit, and the game was won 2-0 thanks to two great goals from Papiss Cisse. There's not much more I can recall about the game due to the amount of alcohol which had passed my lips.

That didn't stop us from heading out on the town straight after the game. We were standing in one bar where a couple of women were having some food. The chips smelled beautiful, and one of them heard me say it. She asked me if I would like one, and without haste I picked one up from her plate and proceeded to dip it in her fried egg. She just smiled at me as I said thank you. Somehow, Bish and I ended up in some nightclub which had three floors. I had drunk so much lager I couldn't face another one. Bish had a great idea of drinking purple WKD. After that, it was my round so I thought cider would be easier to get down. I asked for two bottles of Magners and paid the £8. However, the barmaid gave me six bottles as it was buy one, get two free... Why didn't she tell me that when I ordered? We still managed to drink them.

11/8/12 – Cardiff City Stadium

Newcastle announced a pre-season friendly against Cardiff so another night out was planned in Wales. I drove, and along came Bish, Jonny and French Tony.

Cardiff had just changed the colour of their home kit from blue to red because of their mad owner Vincent Tan. He thinks red is lucky as he is from Malaysia. They moved their blue kit to an away kit, but the owner didn't want it. He didn't understand that the away team must change if there is a clash. He just expected the likes of Man Utd, Liverpool and Arsenal to change their kit to suit him. He wouldn't need to worry about those teams as Cardiff were a Championship side and Newcastle were in the Premier League.

You would not have guessed who the Premier League team was after this performance. Cardiff bossed the game from start to finish and ran out comfortable 4-1 winners. Newcastle's goal came from a Shola Ameobi penalty.

The night out in Cardiff was pleasant. Jonny somehow managed to swap shoes with some girl. She put on one of his Adidas Sambas, while he squeezed into her brown high-heels. We spent most of the night trying to explain English proverbs to French Tony. It all started when Jonny said the girl he had just exchanged footwear with was 'Mutton dressed as Lamb'. This statement blew Tony's mind. To the French, they are the same. After this, we were asking him what the French word was for any random thing. Like at school, he would say it and we would repeat it but we just sounded like when Joey off 'Friends' was learning his French lines for a play. We just kept repeating '*toota le froot*', much to Tony's annoyance.

It was over a year before I ticked off another UK ground as the previous season had seen Newcastle qualify for The Europa League. This meant I visited stadiums in Belgium, France, Ukraine and Portugal instead.

28/8/13 – Globe Arena

When the draw for the Capital One Cup (another new sponsor name…) was made, an away tie at Morecambe meant a Wednesday night trip to the west coast town, again live on Sky TV.

Paul and I were the only ones to make the trip in my trusty MG, but a few other lads were going on the coach. We arrived quite early and parked up in a local school yard which had a sign outside saying Free Football Parking. Then we were told the gates get locked 15 minutes after the final whistle so if the Newcastle supporters were kept back we would be stuck. Instead of risking it we decided to move. However, when I turned the ignition key, nothing. Not a thing. Not even the sound of it trying to start. A quick phone call to my son for guidance and he said something about the immobilizer needing about an hour to reset itself. He informed me just to try it after the game and see what happens. A bit risky, but what other choice did I have?

We walked to have a quick look at the ground, and were quite impressed by the main stand which greeted us. As we were taking a few snaps a bloke in a suit introduced himself to us as a club director, thanked us for coming and took our photo. We walked to the corner of the ground and as it was open, walked straight in. We walked up to the dugouts, took a few photos and left. No-one stopped us, asked us what we were doing, nothing.

We then headed along the sea-front to find the Eric Morecambe statue and more photos.

The Newcastle fans were housed in a terrace behind one goal with a few also in the seats in the main stand. That's where our tickets were for. The attendance was 5,375 which was actually a record highest gate for the stadium. The toon's team was made up of a mixture of experience and youth. Shola Ameobi started on the bench but came on at half time after a goal-less first 45 minutes. He opened the scoring in front of the away fans with only a few minutes left. His younger brother Sammy sealed the win in stoppage time to send the away fans home happy enough. We were not held in the ground at all and headed back to the car wondering if it was going to be a long night. No need to worry as the car started first time. Thank fuck…

I attended a summer pre-season tournament in Schalke, Germany which preceded the start of the 2014-15 season. This came shortly after the tragic events surrounding the Malaysia Airlines flight MH17 where two Newcastle fans were killed, along with 296 others on board, when it was shot down over Ukraine. John Alder and Liam Sweeney were heading to watch Newcastle United play in New Zealand when the unthinkable happened. I had never met Liam but on a few occasions I did meet John. He was nicknamed The Undertaker due to his black suit outfit he wore when watching Newcastle. Eerily, the last time I saw him was on the flight we shared, to and from Ukraine, to watch Newcastle play Metalist Kharkiv in February 2013.

Rest in peace to everyone on that flight.

26/8/14 – Priestfield Stadium

Another Capital One Cup away draw, this time against Gillingham meant another midweek trip. Popularity for this game was fairly low, so I went with Jonny on the 'fun bus'. These are not official coaches but ones where beer and fags, plus some other forms of partyness are allowed, sort of. I was introduced to Beej, a lad from Chester le Street not far from where I live. His name derives from the shortened version of Big John, but not BJ. We set off earlier than normal supporter's coaches do, so we can go to a pre-arranged pub for plenty of beer well before kick-off. As the bus journey took around six hours we had drunk plenty of fluids as it was. Now, geography is not my strongest of subjects and admittedly I did not know where Gillingham is. When I was informed that we would not be home until approx 5am the following morning, I knew I should have booked that day off work. I hastily arranged cover for my morning shift and my start time was moved from 7.30am to 12 noon.

The ground is old school and set in amongst streets of houses. The away section was poor. A temporary stand of seats with no roof, and yes rain was forecast. The other three stands were quite neat and some improvement to the one I was stood on would make it a decent place for everyone to watch football at. The game was probably the dullest I've been to. Newcastle scored in the first half, through an own goal and I don't recall many other chances. Newcastle had loads of possession but were not doing much with the ball in the opposition box. I don't recall any tackles throughout the game either and that showed as there were no yellow cards in the entire 90 minutes.

The long journey back was helped by the usual intake of Fosters and Dark Fruits cider. There was a lad on the bus, who shall be known only as 'Fat Mark'. As we were heading for The Dartford Tunnel, he checked the other scores on his phone to see that Manchester United had been beat 4-0 by MK Dons, and tried to crack up a joke. 'I know their manager is called Louis Van Gaal, but after tonight he will be called Louis Van Gone'. Beej, Jonny and I looked at each other, never cracked a smile, and gazed out of the window. This did not put Fat Mark off as about 30 minutes later; he tried the same joke to some others on the bus, with the same sort of response. All in all, I think I heard that comment six fucking times. I didn't know the lad but Jonny and Beej started to take the piss out of him. He was wearing a white polo shirt with a stain on the bottom at the back. Beej questioned what the stain was off, to be told 'I had a cyst on my back which burst', and I nearly spat Dark Fruits everywhere!!!

The bus dropped us off on the slip road on the A1 at Chester le Street at approx 4.45am. Beej and I said our farewells and headed in opposite directions. My forever-understanding wife Jackie was up for her 6 till 2 shift and picked me up. I told her about Beej walking the couple of miles to his home as well but she turned the car around to take him as well. After we spotted him along the dual carriageway we pulled up alongside and I screamed at him. To say he was slightly startled was an understatement. I hit the pillow around 5.30am with a 10.30am alarm set. It was going to be a long day.

2/12/14 – Turf Moor

Burnley had just been promoted, so theirs was the only ground in the Premier League that I hadn't been to. I made sure I would tick this one off when the fixtures were announced. Stansfield is originally from Burnley so we were hoping for a weekend game in August or April so we could enjoy a stay over, drinking in the sunshine. You guessed it; the fixture computer gave us a Tuesday night game in December!

An early start in a Newcastle bar was the meeting place in order for us to jump on the fun bus leaving at 1pm. Stansfield, Bish, Mick Day and I were met by Jonny, Gary, Beej and a few others I was becoming to know from these trips, just after 11am. You know what kind of trip it's going to be when you've just had your first sip of your first pint and a Jaeger-bomb is shoved into your hand. The bus stopped off at a pre-planned pub approximately half an hour from the ground so we could indulge in pouring more alcohol down our necks, before ferrying us to the ground nearer to kick-off. A large police escort of around ten motorbikes and a few cop-cars delivered us to right outside the away end. I didn't get to see much of the stadium as we were herded straight in. Burnley are another club who seem to up the price of a ticket as soon as Newcastle United come to town, this time charging £40 for a place behind the goal.

Burnley took the lead in the first half, but Papiss Cisse came up trumps with an equalizer just after half time. The game was fairly poor on a bitterly cold night, and the 1-1 draw was just about the fairest result. We trundled back to the bus in order for us to thaw out, and arrived home near the 2 o'clock mark.

29/7/15 – Bootham Crescent

Newcastle had agreed to play a pre-season friendly at League Two side York City on a Wednesday evening so a few crazy people including Jonny, Beej, Sean and I, saw this as a good idea. We jumped on the fun bus and headed down the A19, arriving in plenty of time for refreshments. Our tickets were for an open standing terrace behind the goal, and in typical British summertime fashion, it rained. Newcastle fans accounted for 2,000 of the 5,000 crowd, so it made for a decent atmosphere.

There was a debut for new signing Aleksandar Mitrovic but he was well marshaled by the home defence and didn't get much of a sniff of goal. The hosts went two goals up in the first half and they deserved it. Newcastle fielded a strong side but they were not at the races at all. Newcastle pulled a goal back from Ayoze Perez but it was York City who had high hopes going into the new season, and not the Premier League side.

CHAPTER 5

How Many Left To Do?

During the summer of 2015, I worked out that I had seen a match at 70 English grounds but only 58 were actually still in the league. That meant I had 34 grounds to visit to complete 'The 92'. This is where my journey to random games officially started.

8/8/15 – Spotland

Newcastle's first game of the season was moved back 24 hours due to Southampton playing in Europe so that meant a free Saturday to tick off my next ground. A quick check of the fixtures, and Rochdale v Peterborough in League One was chosen. Bish, Dale and Anth all agreed to come along for the ride and Anth even offered to drive. The four of us stood on the home terrace behind the goal, as part of the 3,300 crowd. Peterborough had Ben Alnwick in goal and as he's an ex-mackem, and brother of Newcastle keeper Jack, he was targeted for light-hearted abuse. I could imagine him thinking 'what is a Geordie accent coming from the Rochdale end all about?' Anyway, the hosts ran out 2-0 winners but I must give credit to the half-time pies, they were very well received.

5/9/15 – Field Mill

International break meant another journey, this time to 'The Oldest Professional Football Ground in the World' so the sign above one stand says. It was Mansfield Town v AFC Wimbledon in League Two.

My old MG had gone to the 'garage in the sky' after clocking up 92,000 miles and numerous away trips, and was replaced by Jackie's 10 year old Renault Clio. She got a new car so I inherited this one. This was its maiden away trip.

Bish, Dale, Singe and I arrived early enough to take in a pint at the ground and, as we were chatting outside in the sunshine, some lass came up to ask about our accents and why we were here. She had overheard us, and recognized our accents as she comes from South Shields originally. She informed us she was the wife of Mansfield Town striker Matt Green, but she didn't seem too happy when we told her we hadn't heard of him and were only here for a trip out.

The one player we had heard about was Wimbledon's man-mountain, Ade Akinfenwa. He was huge, and I still can't believe he could be a professional footballer. Wimbledon took an early lead, but Mansfield soon equalized. That was about as good as it got, and the game ended in a 1-1 draw witnessed by another crowd of just over 3,000.

10/10/15 – Highbury Stadium

Another International break meant a trip to the seaside to Fleetwood Town. Their ground is named Highbury and they play in red, but that's where the similarities with Arsenal ends. They were up against Coventry City in League One, and as Newcastle's Adam Armstrong was there on loan, we decided to go in the away end and support the sky blues. I persuaded my brother-in-law Paul to come along as well as Bish and off we set. We parked very close to the stadium and made our way to the club which is located at the corner of the ground. The fella on the door was confused when he asked if we were home or away fans to which we replied 'Neither'. However, he still wouldn't let us in when we said we had tickets in the away end. He pointed us in the direction of a bar and we duly obliged.

We headed for the away end, and as Paul was wearing a Newcastle top, many people were asking if he was lost. We replied that we had come to watch Adam Armstrong, but imagine our surprise when we were informed he wouldn't be playing as he'd been called up for England Under 19's. The game was very even but in the 90th minute Coventry scored the only goal of the game, to send the 1000 away fans home happy.

After the game, we headed for the fish shop right outside the ground. Now, Fleetwood fans are nicknamed 'The Cod Army' so it was a bit of a shock when we were told they didn't sell cod, only haddock. Anyway, three lots of those were demolished and we journeyed home.

7/11/15 – Dean Court

This season, the only Premier League ground I hadn't been to was Bournemouth, so I knew this was the one trip I would be making. Eugene offered to drive as long as I could sort the tickets, with Bish and Anth up for the trip as well. As Dean Court only holds around 11,000, the away allocation was cut to 1,000. The loyalty point scramble was on and two tickets secured I begged around and Webster (a lad I knew who travelled to a few games on the fun bus) came up trumps.

BT Sport, and not Sky TV for a change, thought it would be a great idea to move the kick-off time forward by a couple of hours to 12.45pm for what was already a six-seven hour journey. We decided on a Friday night stay over so we could see the delights of the Bournemouth night-life, go to the game the following day, and then travel home straight after.

The four of us checked into our hotel, before heading out on the town. We met up with a few of the usual fun bus crew of Jonny, Nat, Sean, Brett, Paul and a few others and enjoyed a few drinks till the early hours. Sean went crazy on the dance floor when the DJ played a Taylor Swift, much to our amusement, and the local's astonishment.

The following day we headed for Dean Court and parked up in a rather posh area, but Eugene's big BMW didn't look out of place. A quick walk to the ground to observe the Remembrance Day minutes silence before kick-off, and hoping for a decent performance. Newcastle took the lead in the first half through Ayoze Perez and then hung on for the next hour. Rob Elliott in the Newcastle goal played a blinder and ensured we took the three points with a 1-0 win, although I've no idea how we managed it.

Back into the car with a two-stop strategy to get us home, taking in the usual sights of motorway services and scoffing down a KFC boneless banquet, we made it back around 10pm.

20/2/16 – Gigg Lane

Newcastle had been knocked out of the FA Cup in the third round (shock…) so I had a free Saturday for another trip. A League One game between Bury and Colchester was selected so Singe, Paul and I jumped into the Clio and headed down the A1. We arrived in decent time and made our way to the ground for a look around, bought our tickets, and went for a pint in the bar attached to the main stand.

You can sit virtually anywhere in the main stand as long as there isn't a season ticket holder sticker on the back of the seat so we sat in the front row of the upper tier. In front of us used to be terracing but this has long since been disused and is now covered with advertising banners. Paul needed the toilet so as we were stood beside the dugout area, I said to Singe, 'Let's get a photo in the dugout' and walked off down the steps with Singe nervously following, both of us giggling like naughty school kids. We reached the side of the pitch where one of the young Colchester substitutes was warming up, and we got him to take our photo before casually walking back to our seats.

Colchester, who had ex-Newcastle player Darren Ambrose in the side, raced into a two-goal lead before having a player sent off for two yellows after half an hour. Bury pulled one back almost immediately and the crowd sensed a second half comeback. They weren't disappointed when Bury midfielder Andrew Tutte hit a second half hat-trick which saw Bury eventually run out comfortable 5-2 winners.

25/3/16 – Sixfields Stadium

Easter weekend is always a great time to tick off a lower league game as there are loads to choose from. Good Friday meant a journey to see Northampton v Newport in League Two with

Anth offering his services as driver, with Singe and Bish making up the car full. Sixfields was in the process of being redeveloped, with a partially built new stand running down the opposite side of the pitch. We approached one of the stewards and told him about our journey and asked for a dugout photo. Quick as a flash he escorted us pitchside and we got the photo. From there we headed for Carr's Bar, named after the Newcastle scout Graham Carr, who also played for and managed Northampton. Both sets of fans mingled with each other before time to take our seats. Even though Northampton were on their way to winning the division while Newport were just above the drop zone, the game was fairly even. However, Northampton took the points with a 1-0 win in front of a decent attendance of over 5,000.

28/3/16 – Vale Park

Bank Holiday Monday was a trip to Port Vale for the second game of my Easter double-header. This time I drove, with Paul and Dale coming along for the ride.

We got to the ground fairly early so bought our tickets straight away. Next to the ticket office was a large gate where a head steward was giving out a pre-match briefing to the other stewards. I waited till he had finished before asking for a dugout photo. He was really puzzled when I explained where we were from, but he showed us around and took the photo. We then headed to the local bar not far from the ground for a pint before kick-off. In contrast to Friday's game, it was the away side Barnsley who were pushing for promotion with Vale mid-table. Barnsley had youngster Ivan Toney on loan from Newcastle so it was a chance to see if he showed any glimpses of skill, while in goal for Port Vale was ex-Newcastle player Jak Alnwick. Just under 5,000 saw another tight game but the away side just shaded it 1-0. Alnwick couldn't do much about the Barnsley goal, and all Toney had to show for his workout was a yellow card, before being substituted.

CHAPTER 6

Another Championship Season

25/7/16 – Roots Hall

Newcastle had suffered another horrible relegation at the end of the last season, which meant another year in The Championship. However, this did mean I had the chance of ticking off a few more grounds with Newcastle, instead of random trips away.

A pre-season friendly against Southend United on a Tuesday night wasn't great but as I hadn't been there it had to be done. Singe and I had booked on a 'Fat Mark's fun bus leaving from Newcastle, with us getting picked up on the A1 slip-road at Chester le Street at 10am. We got there in plenty of time and waited. And we waited. And we waited. I rang John Yates, who I knew was going as well, and he informed me the bus hadn't left yet as only six people out of the 30 who expressed an interest had turned up. He was desperately trying to arrange for a minibus instead of a huge coach to take us but the prices they were quoting was astronomical. After an hour or so, the decision to call the trip off was made by John, so Singe and I considered our options. The only option we had was to go home, jump in my trusty Clio and head south for a six hour drive.

When we got there, we headed for a steward to ask about the possibility of a dugout photo, and he agreed without a problem. He took us down and we got the snap we desired, or even deserved. As we were walking out, some of the Newcastle squad walked out onto the pitch and the first one I grabbed hold of was 'Ginger' Jack Colback. He posed for a photo with me, and then Singe and we headed outside. From there we saw the team bus, so decided just to walk on board. The driver stopped us from going on as the players had left some of their personal items on it, but he did allow for a quick video so I could always say I'd been on it.

When it was near to kick off we headed into the ground for a bite to eat and chose the usual 'football ground pie'. This pie was the hottest pie in the world, cooked in a volcano near to Southend, and took about half an hour for it to come down to a normal edible temperature. Inside the ground and I meet up with old friends Stan Baker and his son, as well as Paul Dinning.

6,500 were in attendance which included around 1,000 travelling Geordies, and they saw Newcastle run out 2-0 winners thanks to second-half goals from Anita and Gouffran. There was also a debut for recent signing Grant Hanley.

The six hour journey home was going great until overnight closures of the A1 at Scotch Corner sent us via Barnard Castle, Bishop Auckland and other random Durham pit villages. We arrived home around 4.30am and I went straight to bed. Singe however had to be up for work in two hours.

20/8/16 – Ashton Gate

Newcastle had started the season with two defeats before picking up their first win at home on the Wednesday night. The first league away trip for me was Bristol City. We went on the fun bus with Jonny, Nat, Sean, John Yates, Beej and others setting off at a ridiculous time of 6am. Now, my personal rules of not opening a can of beer until you get past the cherry-pickers was in force so I had my first can of Fosters at 6.15am. It was going to be a long day.

We got to Bristol and outside the ground was a fan-zone where fans from both teams were chatting. The rain started to fall so any cover was premium. We headed into the ground, not before Beej and I posed for a photo at the player's entrance. The sign above said 'Home of Bristol City & Bristol Rugby', the size of us didn't fool anyone into believing we were anything other than fat football fans, and definitely not egg-chasers.

Our seats were in line with the corner flag looking up towards the dugouts on the right. Dwight Gayle finished off a well worked goal to put Newcastle in front at half-time. At the interval, I headed down to near the corner flag for a couple of moments but then the steward in attendance walked away leaving a free gap for me to exploit. I walked towards the dugouts when this huge security guard stopped me and threatened to have me kick out for being there. I pleaded my innocence and explained my quest for a photo in every dugout. The steward told me to come back after the game and he would see what he could do.

The second half saw Bristol City up the pressure but Newcastle held on to record a fine victory. I told Sean of my photo opportunity, and he accompanied me for our photo before heading back onto the coach for the long journey home.

3/9/16 – Gresty Road

The first International break of the season gave me an opportunity to see Crewe Alexandra play Doncaster Rovers in League Two. I emailed Crewe a few days earlier to inform them of our journey and request for a dugout photo, to which they agreed. Anth came up trumps with the offer of driving and Bish made up the trio.

When we arrived, we were escorted down towards the tunnel past the changing rooms, out onto the pitchside. The dugouts are not really dugouts, but a small section of blue seats set amongst the red seats of the main stand with railings around them to separate the fans from the players and staff. The ground is made up of the fairly impressive main stand as well as three smaller stands. The name of the stand opposite is strangely called 'The Ice Cream Van Stand'.

Just less than 4,000 people saw Crewe take a half time lead, but Doncaster were awarded a penalty with around ten minutes left in which they looked like they had snatched a point. However, with time running out, Crewe scored again to take the points in a 2-1 win.

1/10/16 – New York Stadium

I never went to Rotherham's previous home of Millmoor but I did see them play at their temporary home of The Don Valley Stadium which they used while this new stadium was being built. Once again, I ventured to this ground in the fun bus with Jonny, Nat, Beej and the likes. A nice short journey compared to some of the ones endured this season.

Rotherham threw everything at Newcastle in this game, but one piece of skill from Christian Atsu just before half time gave the toon a very important three points with a 1-0 win.

12/11/16 – Blundell Park

As it was an international break I planned a trip to Grimsby. This was the shortest trip of the grounds I had left to tick off, so I rounded up Bish and Paul, a couple of mates who I have been dragging around England for the last couple of seasons, in order to reduce the fuel costs. Then I get a call from Nipper, a mate who lives nearby who is can-you-believe, a Tottenham Hotspur season ticket holder….. this man is approximately 8 grounds ahead of me in his list of 'doing the 92', and the amount of miles he does every weekend travelling to watch Spurs play home and away is nothing short amazing (or mad!!). He is at a loose end and since he hasn't ticket off Blundell Park, asks to come along for the ride. Great, four of us for the trip, I thought. Another message from one of my other mates Gavin, and he asks 'is there room in the car for me?' Now five fully grown blokes in a Renault Clio is something you don't expect to see, but we all squeezed in and set off. I have attempted to get a photo in the dug-out of most of the grounds I visit, and this usually means I speak to a friendly steward who understands what I'm doing, quickly walk in, photo, and quickly walk back out. We arrived early, just as the Barnet team bus pulled up, and I asked the steward who is at the player's entrance my question. Now, I think he must have believed we were with the away team, as without a moment's hesitation he shows us in. We get our photo, wander down the tunnel, peak into the away dressing room, and then speak to the stadium manager. We ask him how to get to the ticket office, to which he tells us 'you are in now so just go for a pint in the bar and sit at the back of the stand when kick off nears'. Not very often you get in for nowt!! Apart from Nipper, that is. He had already booked and paid for his ticket online when it was confirmed he could go.

The game was a decent match. Grimsby raced into a two goal half time lead, but were pegged back with two Barnet penalties. Grimsby were awarded penalty of their own in the 90th minute but Omar Bogle, who scored twice in the first half, smashes it over the bar. The game had goals; penalties scored and missed, and even a sending off.

Now a trip to Cleethorpes can't be complete without fish & chips, so we found a recommended place to eat, and tucked into our bait before heading home. All in all, a good day out.

3/12/16 – Proact Stadium

I had found myself with a spare Saturday to tick off another ground.

Three of us, Paul, Anth and I, jumped into my trusty old Clio and headed approx. 150 miles south to Chesterfield's Proact Stadium to make it 69 out of 92 for me. There was an FA Cup 2nd Round tie taking place, with the added lure of a ticket for only a tenna. As usual we got there early to attempt our dugout photo. We parked in the stadium car park for £7, a bit steep considering the price of a ticket. We were allowed in for a photo, and escorted through the player's entrance and down the tunnel (always a bonus) and the photos were taken. We made our way back out of the stadium, and found a pub right outside the ground till kick off neared.

With only 30 minutes till kick off, we headed inside the stadium to sample the pies, and read the programme. The pie was so hot, it was impossible to taste. The programme was poor. It was wafer thin and cost £2. I don't know whether this was because of the low profile cup match or not. The match itself was a struggling League One side at home to a mid-table League Two side. If you didn't know which team were which, you could quite easily have got them wrong! Wycombe easily won 5-0. Fair play to the travelling fans as they never stopped singing (and banging their f*cking drum!) all game. After the half time interval, as Wycombe's striker Adebayo Akinfenwa, who had signed from Wimbledon in the summer, came back out onto the pitch, I shouted at him and called him 'Fatty'. His response was a huge smile in my direction. At the end of the game I waited near the dugout in order to ask 'Fatty' for a photo. He duly obliged, not before he gave me a bear-hug. I soon realised there wasn't an ounce of fat on him, just pure muscle. Such a great sport, no wonder he has legendary status wherever he plays.

17/12/16 – Pirelli Stadium

It was another fun bus trip to see Newcastle's first ever visit to Burton Albion's stadium. The usual crew of Jonny, Nat, Sean, John Yates, Beej, Paul Mac, Brett and others made the journey on a cold Saturday just before Christmas.

The ground is one of the smallest grounds I've ever seen Newcastle play at, but the 1,700 Geordies and the 5,000 or so home fans made it a decent atmosphere. Another thing we've missed out on recently was the chance to stand on a terrace behind a goal. This removes the cuts and bruises to the shins following any goal celebrations from the seats in front.

Newcastle took the lead when Dwight Gayle scored right in front of the away fans. We were soon pegged back but Mo Diame put us back into the lead when he calmly passed the ball into the net, before half time. The second half was as expected and the toon withstood any home pressure and took the points. The 'Jingle Bells' song about seeing Newcastle win away belted out as the fans made our way out. I stopped to ask a steward for a quick photo in the dugout before we left, and to my surprise he said yes. I grabbed hold of Brett to join me in the photo before heading back to the coach, clambering on board just as it was about to leave.

14/1/17 – Griffin Park

The old Clio was the mode of transport for this drive to London, with Paul and Singe jumping in as well. We arrived fairly early and parked up in an underground car park not far from the ground. Brentford's ground is known for having a pub on each corner, and we made our way to 'The Griffin' as it was near to the away section. We nearly didn't get to see the game because on the walk there, some crazy woman came hurtling around the corner like it was Formula One and just missed Singe by inches. I had some tickets for lads who were to meet us outside the pub, including a Chinese lad called Shawn (yeah, right!) who had contacted me via Twitter, and a couple were for John Yates who had travelled on the fun bus. Singe went to the bar and I asked for a pint of real ale if they had one. I don't know what it was called but it tasted like it had been dredged from the Thames and pumped directly to the pub. I still drank it, though. Paul decided to go to place around the back of the pub which was selling cans instead of queuing inside. He bought three cans except he was given two 500ml cans and one 440ml can. Seeing a bloke argue about 60ml of Strongbow cider is quite entertaining, however he was charged £4 for each one!

Shawn arrived to collect his ticket and decided to tag along with us as he was by himself, but John Yates didn't appear and his phone was going straight to voicemail. We headed to the ground with around fifteen minutes to kick off when I spot John pacing up and down the turnstiles. The look on his face when he saw me was one of pure love, or relief.

This was the second game where standing on a terrace was permitted. Added to the fact there was a low roof with seats in the stand above made for great noise from around 1500 away fans. There was a minute's applause in memory of ex-England manager Graham Taylor who had passed away during the week just before kick-off.

Newcastle took a first half lead when Dwight Gayle kept up his decent run of goals by scoring in front of the away fans, before limping off minutes later. Brentford equalised in the second half but Darryl Murphy scored a header at the far end to make it 2-1 to the toon with ten minutes left. A huge sigh of disapproval greeted the nine minutes of added time being indicated by the fourth official, but some Keystone Cops defending by Lascelles, Clark and Dummett ensured another three points would be coming home with us.

Walking back to the car we stopped off at a Morrison's to grab some food before setting off. Now Singe, who is from Stanley, bought a crayfish and avocado sandwich. Nobody from Stanley has ever heard of crayfish or avocado, never mind buys it. We got back to the underground car park where we had our second near miss. A huge Range Rover drove down through the exit ramp where we were walking and parked up in a residential parking area. Singe needed a piss before the journey so got one up against a pillar only for the big bloke from the Range Rover to have a go at him. It's obvious the bloke didn't understand our Geordie accents, as he told us not to do that round here, its not Romania or Poland you know. Wow, racially abused in our own country!

28/1/17 – Kassam Stadium

Newcastle had been drawn away to Oxford United in the FA Cup fourth round so as I hadn't been there, it was a definite. Brothers-in-law Paul and Ray came along, as did an old mate of mine called Phil Rooney, and the Clio was on the road once again. I had read that car parking was very scarce around the ground as were pubs. We got there early enough to get a space and headed for the ground to request a dugout photo. Job done, we walked to the nearby bowling alley which served beer. I think the whole of Oxford had the same idea as the place was packed. The Kassam Stadium is made up of three stands with only a large car park behind the goal to our right. This is the only ground I've been to where I could see my car from my seat. The Newcastle side was made up of reserve/fringe players as well as a couple of young'uns, but did have Mitrovic and Perez up front. The first half was quite poor but Mitrovic was guilty of missing a couple of decent chances. The second half was less than a minute old when Oxford scored. Mitrovic had the chance to equalise from the penalty spot but his effort was easily saved by the keeper. Oxford scored again with 10 minutes left before sealing the game with a third in the dying minutes. The only action we saw was a couple of Newcastle fans fighting amongst themselves after the final whistle.

We were all disappointed with the performance, losing to a side from a division below in the cup again. Just like Stevenage and Brighton from previous trips. We decided to head back to the Bowling place to let the traffic die down, and so the lads could let of some steam over a pint. We walked in and one jubilant home fan thought he was clever by asking Ray what the score was. Ray replied by saying 'ask me that again and I'll knock your teeth out'. The Oxford fan didn't ask it again but wisely moved to another part of the bar. We set off for home in what was a fairly quiet car this time.

10/2/17 – Rodney Parade

Newport County's Rodney Parade was a ground I was going to leave till late in my quest to do the 92 as I feared they may be one team to fall through the trapdoor into Non-League. However, when I spotted their game against Doncaster Rovers had been moved to a Friday night I quickly scoured the fixture list for a possible double-header weekend. Thankfully, Bristol Rovers were playing at home on the Saturday so my mind was quickly made up to tick off two grounds in one weekend. When its 300 miles one way, it's always bonus to get two ticked off.

I managed to persuade three mates, Paul, Bish and Gavin, to agree to the trip away, booked the hotel and awaited the day to arrive. During the week before the trip I looked online to read up on the selected matches. To my amazement, the referee selected for the Newport match was David Webb, a friend of mine who lives only three miles from me. I sent him a text to confirm this with him, and the offer of going for a pint after the game. Sadly, he declined my offer as he was driving part of the way home after the match, but he came up trumps with the offer of four free tickets for me and my mates… result!!

We set off for Wales on the Friday at 11am and arrived at the hotel at 5.30pm. After dropping our bags off, we set off to pick up our tickets. We arrived just under two hours before kick-off, plenty of time to get the customary dugout photo sorted without too much of a problem. Our tickets were for 'The 100 club' executive lounge. Four pints were ordered, served in real pint glasses, total £13.00. Not too bad. The steward who was on duty in this area was fantastic. We chatted for about 30 minutes until it started to fill up. A couple of pints later, and it was match time. The ground itself was made up of an old style stand with seats above a terrace. Facing that was the most modern stand. This is where we were; a number of corporate boxes with multi coloured seats in front. To either end of the pitch was open terracing, but not many fans braved these areas on a cold night. The pitch was awful, resembling a beach with pale green areas dotted around the outskirts. As this was top v bottom in League Two we all agreed this would be a leveller.

Sure enough, the game was as poor as the pitch. The game started well with Newport having a decent chance within 90 seconds. Doncaster had a few chances of their own but both defences were playing well. As the temperature dropped to near freezing point, my mate blew the final whistle to bring to an end a drab game 0-0.

After the game we stayed in the bar area for another pint waiting for the officials to come out, when the steward said he would take us down to the tunnel area. We got some photos and thanked the man-in-the-middle for the free tickets, before heading into the town centre for a couple more beers. We were informed to try out Potters Bar, which had a live band playing and a clientele of similar aged people to us. No rowdy boom-boom music or lager-louts in sight. We stayed till 1am then set off for a pizza. The pizza was probably the worst I have ever tasted, but that didn't stop me from finishing it. We headed back to our digs having had a great day.

11/2/17 – Memorial Stadium

The four of us woke up rather groggy from the night before but we all managed breakfast. We checked out and set off eastwards back to England. We arrived at Bristol Rovers Memorial Stadium, and parked on the nearby Muller Road. We headed to the ground at 11.30am to ask for a dugout photo. No problems there and we were duly escorted pitch side by a senior steward. While chatting to the steward we mentioned how we were given free tickets for last night's Newport match (failing to mention they were off a mate). Not to be out-done by a League Two club, he asked us to wait near the dugouts and he 'would see what he could do'.

As we were standing alone near the pitch two rather official looking men in Bristol Rovers suits and coats asked us what we were doing. Again, we mentioned our quest 'doing the 92' and the fact we had travelled 300 miles from the North East. This is when the unbelievable happened. They showed us the corporate facilities in the East stand, which were quite impressive. From the outside the stand looked odd only covering the middle third of the pitch but with a terrace running the full length. We were then taken across to the main stand. We were escorted down the tunnel and introduced to the Bristol Rovers manager Darrel Clarke. Following that we went into the home dressing room and chatted with ex-Sunderland player Marcus Stewart who is the Assistant Manager. Even as a Newcastle fan, I shook his hand and thanked him for his time. A quick peek into the away dressing room was followed by a look upstairs to the chairman's box. This was by far so much more than anything we could have expected. On the way back out, we were handed four complimentary tickets for the terrace behind the dugouts. We were told to enjoy 'Irene's Kitchen', a bar and food service area with TV's showing the early kick off. There are signs up which state 'no away fans' and we were questioned about this when they heard our Geordie accents. I only had coffee as I had 300+ miles to drive but the others sampled the beer. The food on offer looked decent, not too pricey. There were burgers, bacon rolls, chips etc all on offer. However, we all agreed to save ourselves for a pasty on the terraces. The pasty was £3.20 and in all honesty, a bit on the dear side and a bit dry for my liking.

The match itself was a decent affair. Rovers opened the scoring when Chris Lines curled in a left foot effort from outside the box. Cue a chant of 'he's one of our own' from the Rovers faithful behind the goal. Nicky Law equalised about ten minutes later after some neat build up play. The second half saw Bradford have more attacking chances but the Rovers keeper was in good form and a draw was probably a fair result, with most of the 9,000 crowd going home content.

We set off for home having been to two countries in two days, seeing two goals during two draws. After I had dropped everyone off their respective homes, the total round trip came to 642 miles added to the Clio. Well worth it.

25/3/17 – Abbey Stadium

As it was the international break for the top two divisions, including my beloved Newcastle United, I decided this was the perfect time to tick off another ground. The usual text message to my mates asking if they fancied 'a random' wasn't received as well as hoped; hardly surprising as it's only me who's interested in completing the 92. Fortunately, my brother-in-law Paul said yes, so I wasn't going it alone. The next part of the plan was to see where we were going to end up. The nearest grounds left to do were identified as Walsall or Shrewsbury. A little further afield, there was the lure of seeing ex-Newcastle players Shola Ameobi, Adam Campbell and Alan Smith play for Kevin Nolan's Notts County away at Wycombe Wanderers. We decided to keep the fuel costs down we would go to Walsall. However, due to Walsall having international players from Philippines, Afghanistan, Cyprus and Canada all receiving call-ups, this game was called off. Next choice was Shrewsbury. Once again, our plan was scuppered due to this game being declared all-ticket, and if you hadn't registered with the club previous to the announcement, you couldn't buy a ticket. We then decided on Cambridge and waited to see if anything would cause us to change our plans again… Match day arrived without any further alterations and we started the day by tucking away a fantastic cooked breakfast served up by my better half. We set off on the 230 mile journey south down the A1. Just under four hours later we arrived at our destination. I parked in a side street within sight of the floodlights and we headed towards the ground. I asked for our usual dugout photo and even got the bonus mascot photo with 'Marvin the Moose'. We then headed into 'The Dion Dublin Bar' for a pint. Just under £8 for a couple of pints served in actual glasses seemed a little over-priced but that's what you get at most grounds now. The only thing wrong with this bar was the annoying chat of the compère from the neighboring hospitality suite being pumped in through the speakers. We finished our pints and headed for The Abbey Lounge, only to be turned away as we weren't members. We decided to head into the stadium to find a few bars selling a range of burgers etc and a bottle bar selling alcohol and soft drinks. £3.70 for a bottle of beer was pricey as well.

We bought our tickets for The North Habbin Stand; £16 to stand along the side of the pitch was decent value, as long as you bought your tickets in advance. Only half of the stand was open, as the south part of the stand is used for overspill for the away fans. To our left was the home end which housed 'The Amber Army'. This was the only area of noise from the home support. The opposite end housed the away fans and fair play to them for making a decent bit of noise; although the drum banging did help. The main stand had all the character of an 'old school' stand.

The game itself wasn't great; some blood and guts challenges were the only things to cheer about. There weren't many chances created and I can only recall about five shots in the whole game. After the game, we decided to let the traffic die down and headed for fish & chips. A huge fish and perfect chips were duly devoured before the long journey home. I arrived back just before 10pm, having added another 464 miles to my trusty Clio.

17/4/17 – Portman Road

Easter Monday was to be my last Newcastle away trip of the season, travelling to Ipswich Town. Paul came along and brought his two sons for the occasion celebrated as 'Sir Bobby Robson Day'.

The journey down wasn't too bad considering it was around a four-hour drive for yours truly. We arrived at a nearby car-park, only about 400 yards from the ground, and walked around the stadium. The 'Ipswich Town FC' lettering on the outside of the main stand overlooked a large area where there were plenty of activities going on. However, strangely, they are for home fans only. We carried on our walk and came across the Sir Bobby Robson Stand, which sits behind one of the goals. At the corner of this stand is a statue, but not of Sir Bobby, but of Sir Alf Ramsey. Opposite the Cobbold Stand is a statue of Sir Bobby Robson, to which there was the dreaded half and half scarf draped around his shoulders. I really hate those scarves. The Sir Alf Ramsey Stand which is behind the other goal makes up a decent ground which hosted their glory days back in the early 80's. I still think the statues need re-housed. From here we headed to a bar across the river, which the away following had taken over, until it was time for the game to start.

As usual, a match day programme was purchased, but for this game the price had increased from £3 to £4 to mark the occasion. We had already paid just short of £40 for a ticket so what's an extra quid?

On a day when Newcastle were pushing for the title they just didn't get started. Ipswich went in front just before half time following a mistake by Matt Ritchie. The Toon equalised when former Ipswich player Darryl Murphy scored. However, there was no celebration from him but the away fans went mental. Those celebrations were short lived as another error, this time from Karl Darlow, gifted Ipswich the lead again. In stoppage time the game was over when the hosts scored their third.

We trudged back to the car park, and sat in a queue for ages before eventually getting onto the open road. The only thing I had to look forward to now was a KFC Boneless Banquet.

22/4/17 – Kenilworth Road

With Newcastle United's match at home to Preston moved to the Monday night, it gave me a free Saturday and a possibility to tick off another ground in my quest for 'The 92'. On the Wednesday before, a quick check of the referee appointments for that weekend to see where my mate would be posted, showed he had been given Luton Town v Notts County. I hadn't been there…

My text to Mr Webb was replied to with the offer of free travel and tickets, but I would need to book a room at the hotel he was staying in, and be able to travel on the Friday evening. I hastily contacted my brother-in-law Paul to see if he was available. He was, but I needed to sweet-talk my better half as I had just returned from Ipswich Town two days earlier. I got an ear-bashing, but she succumbed to my begging and granted me another night away.

We were picked up by David at 8pm on the Friday and spent the next four hours heading south to Luton. This time was spent discussing the life of a referee, and I can honestly say what an incredible insight we were given. Not many football fans will realise the level of commitment referees, and their assistants, give to our beautiful game.

Every game for the officials is an 'away game'. Without really thinking about it, we all assume they are teleported into the stadium. We spent some time discussing the laws of the game and 'what if this happened' questions, before arriving at the hotel around midnight. David headed straight to bed while Paul and I headed for the bar. At around 2am we hit the sack ready for a 9am breakfast rendezvous.

On the morning of the game, we set off for Kenilworth Road and arrived around mid-day. We were met by former league linesman and now Luton Town match-day host Matt Buonassisi. We were then given our complimentary tickets and escorted into the officials changing rooms. From there we were taken across the pitch for our customary dugout photo, this time including the ref!!

Whilst on the pitch more photos were taken to record something loads of Luton Town fans would love to do, just to be on the pitch. We realised then, what a privileged position we were in. We headed back inside, and sat in the 'John Moore Lounge', named after the former Luton player and manager, for coffee and sandwiches waiting for the other officials to arrive. The two referee's assistants, the fourth official, the referee's assessor, and even the assessor's boss all arrived and chatted informally with us about our love of all things Newcastle United. This didn't seem to interest our Sunderland fan referee. At 1.30pm the officials made their way to the changing rooms, which signaled time for a pint.

Talking about betting and drinking alcohol is strictly forbidden when sitting in the company of any match official. A couple of pints of reasonably priced ale soon disappeared and it was time for kick off. We went to our seats and sat only a dozen or so seats away from Luton chairman and TV presenter Nick Owen.

Notts County, whose starting line-up included Geordie cult hero Shola Ameobi and ex-toon player Adam Campbell, started the brighter; the magpies going ahead within six minutes with a fine finish from Elliott Hewitt. Luton levelled ten minutes later when Danny Hylton smashed a curler off the bar and Ollie Palmer reacted quickest to head home. On the stroke of half time The Hatters took the lead when Pelly Ruddock scored from the edge of the area. The second half saw both sides create chances, but to be denied by some good goal keeping at each end. The talking point was the red card for Luton striker Danny Hylton. In the first half he was booked for jumping into the County keeper, and in stoppage time he was warned when not retreating the full ten yards for a free kick. Moments later he put another late challenge in to give the man in the middle no option but to send him off. Later, in the tunnel area Hylton didn't seem too displeased with his enforced suspension, knowing he would be back in time for the play-offs.

With the game over, we made our way back to the John Moore lounge to watch the final scores coming in from around the leagues. We were then escorted to near the changing rooms to wait for David. Once there, we waited like excited school kids hoping for that moment when you meet your hero. First out was the Notts County manager, and hat-trick hero of Newcastle's 5-1 demolition of Sunderland back in 2010, Kevin Nolan. A couple of handshakes and photos later and he was back inside for a drink with the home manager.

Next up was the scorer of Newcastle's other two goals in that memorable match against our bitter rivals, Shola Ameobi. What a great fella he is. He chatted with us for a couple of minutes, thanking us for our support for him, and our love for the toon. We could have stayed longer but we knew the referee, and our chauffeur, had another four-hour drive to complete.

We arrived home around 10.15pm. I was still buzzing from a great day, but for David Webb it was just another day at the office.

CHAPTER 7

The Home Straight

5/8/17 – The New Meadow

I had eagerly awaited the start of the season, as I had calculated that with only 16 more grounds to tick off, I would aim to complete my quest. My mate David Webb had been appointed referee at Oldham for the opening game of the season, so I would need to search again. My mind was quickly made up when Webby sent a text saying another referee mate of his Seb Stockbridge, was in charge at Shrewsbury Town that day and two guest tickets were on offer. Offer accepted.

Paul and I headed down the A1 as usual but just as we arrived there was a huge thunderstorm and the rain was bouncing as high as it was falling. I feared the game could be called off due to a waterlogged pitch with the amount that was coming down. As we got to the ground car park, I told the drenched attendant we were guests of the referee but did not have any passes. Not a problem, we were told to park in a certain area and that was that. We headed to pick up the tickets and were directed to where all the match officials were sitting. The offer of coffee, biscuits and sandwiches was well received. Seb took us down the tunnel for our dugout photo, before he and the other officials had to leave us. We stayed in the players and officials area until near to kick off, before heading to our seats.

The game was a tight affair and looked to be heading for the unwanted 0-0 draw, but in the 92nd minute a Shrewsbury Town substitute scrambled the ball home to snatch the points.

19/8/17 – The New Lawn

On Monday evening I received a text message which contained three words. Those words were 'Forest Green Saturday'. The text was from my referee mate David Webb, who was helping me achieve my goal of reaching 'The 92 Club'.

As I had agreed to work on the Saturday in question, I had two people who I needed to persuade. The first was a colleague to cover my shift. The second, but more importantly, was the wife. Both of these obstacles were successfully navigated, which meant a trip away on the Friday night staying in Bromsgrove. As ever on these trips, my trusty side-kick Paul, came along. David picked us up at 7.30pm on the Friday, and we set off on the 4 hour drive south. Halfway, we stopped off for a coffee at a service station, where we had a pre-arranged meeting with another ref on his travels, Seb Stockbridge. Seb was on his way to referee the following day's game at Luton Town.

We arrived at the hotel around 11.30pm and by 11.35pm we were in the bar. Sadly, David couldn't join us so we forced down a few pints of overly-priced Stella Artois, and retired around the 2.30am mark. We knew we had a cooked breakfast to destroy at 9am.

The match-day breakfast was as expected, excellent. Paul managed three large sausages as well as the usual bacon, mushrooms, hash browns, black pudding, eggs, beans and toast. He is quite fond of a sausage is our Paul. I think he was concerned about the lack of meat on sale at The New Lawn.

We travelled to The New Lawn, arriving slightly earlier than planned. The route took us through the lovely Gloucestershire countryside, down many narrow roads with only a few passing places slowing us down.

We headed for the players and officials entrance, which surprisingly is not near the main reception, but in the far corner of the stadium. The teams enter the field from this corner and walk across the pitch towards the dugouts in the main stand. A little peak into the home dressing room, revealed a bright vibrant green colour. A check of the strips of the opponents Yeovil Town, who were also playing in their green, showed not too much of a clash to cause any problems.

The main stand is a decent size; however the two terraced stands behind each goal are fairly typical for this level. The away fans are housed in the uncovered section running alongside the pitch.

This is a change from last season as the away fans used to stand behind the goal to the right of the main stand.

We headed across to the main stand to wait in the Director's Suite until the rest of the officials arrived. However, on the way, we needed to stop at the dugouts for our customary photo. We were given a choice of drinks, but as were in the company of officials, it's hot or soft drinks only. I asked for coffee with milk; soya milk was served.

The food menu is littered with many offerings, all vegan. When the officials made their way to the changing rooms at 1.30pm, we headed for the bar. We went to the Carol Embrey Suite, which is located at the rear of the East Stand. I thought the food prices being charged for the fans were a little high. A vegan pie, pasty, burger or wrap with chips would set you back £7.00.

A number of brands of beers are not sold at The New Lawn, such as Guinness & John Smiths due to their brewing techniques involving animal extracts etc. However, a local Stroud Brewery had a number of ales on sale including the one we had, a hand-pulled real ale called Buddlings priced at £3.90. A couple of pints later, it was match time.

We sat in the second row, towards the right of the pitch level with the 18 yard box. I know it is early in the season but the pitch looked remarkable. Remember, there are no fertilizers used at all on the pitch, and it is watered using collected rain water.

The game itself saw Yeovil take an early lead, before our mate in the middle pointed to the spot to allow the away side to double it. It was probably the easiest penalty he has ever given, no arguments from any of the defenders. Forest Green pulled a goal back before Yeovil scored again. Just before half time, Rovers scored direct from a free kick. '3-1 and you fucked it up' was the chant as the home side scored two more goals in the second half, to claim their first ever Football League victory.

Another pint after the game was taken while we waited for our mate to get showered and changed. Whilst there, the Man of the Match presentation took place. Bigger clubs do this in their corporate areas away from genuine fans, but this was just another little thing which set them apart from other clubs.

We set off on the journey, and had only travelled roughly 10 miles before Paul had succumbed to the excitement of seeing seven goals, and nodded off in the back seat. Just as well the driver didn't. After all, it was him who had run around for 90 minutes! The 270 mile homeward bound trip was interrupted with the A1 being closed. This diversion added another 45 minutes to the timescale. We arrived back home at 11pm and I was happy in the knowledge I had reached number 78/92.

2/9/17 – Sincil Bank

Lincoln City had just been promoted to The Football League so this was a fairly local game considering what I had left to do. Once again Paul came along, as did Gavin. We arrived early to collect our tickets and then proceeded to get a photo in the dugout. The away team was Luton Town and they had quite a large following which bumped the attendance to over 9,000.
The game was another even affair with a couple of chances for each side which came to nothing. Sadly, there were no goals but the atmosphere was decent.

23/9/17 – The Hive

Barnet were next on the list as they were playing Crawley Town in League Two. Webby had emailed the ref for this game Darren Handley, regarding tickets but he never replied. It was a drive to London with Paul for this mammoth game. The fact that Barnet's attendances are regularly low meant we could probably choose to sit anywhere. We decided to stand behind the goal with the hardcore home fans paying £19. We were in and out for dugout photo with no problems, and then watched the early kick off match in the bar situated within the main stand. The game on the big screen was West Ham v Tottenham and I couldn't help but wonder why the fans were cheering every Spurs goal. I asked a bloke in the bar about this and his reply was that for a lot of the 'fans' who come here, Barnet are their second club and they can't get, or afford, tickets for Spurs.

The first half of the game was poor, and I recall commenting on the number of tube trains that passed the corner of the ground, so much was the standard of play. It came to life in the second half when Crawley scored. Barnet equalised soon after but were hit with a sucker-punch when Crawley scored again in the 89th minute.

The official attendance was a low count of 1,602. I believe Paul and I were the two.

7/10/17 – Stadium MK

An email from Virgin Trains with the offer of cheap first class travel ignited an idea to tick off a ground in the capital and allow me to enjoy the journey instead of a four hour drive each way. I persuaded my trusty side-kick Paul to come along too. We decided on the international break weekend and duly booked up the train in order to visit Charlton Athletic and tick off the Valley.

However a week before our trip, Charlton's match was called off due to a number of players being selected for their relevant countries. With train tickets paid for this meant a look at which ground we could visit instead. Considering I only had 12 to do to complete 'the 92', it made the task rather difficult.

The train tickets were non-refundable so desperation started to set in when none of the teams I had left to do in the locality were playing at home. The nearest one to London was Milton Keynes Dons, so we decided on their game against Bradford City. Unfortunately this meant further expense as we would need to get another train to get there, best laid plans and all that!

The morning of the match arrived and we travelled in first class luxury. We arrived into Kings Cross at 12.45, walked to Euston Station to catch the 1.15 train to Bletchley, passing the Wembley Arch along the way. From there we jumped in a taxi and arrived at the ground just after 2pm. We headed to the box office and paid £22 to sit behind the goal. It was 'Armed Forces Day' at the stadium, so there were a number of displays around to keep the younger fans amused.

We decided to head inside to view the stadium, and I must say we were very impressed. Such a great stadium should not be hosting third tier football. Every one of the 32,000 seats were padded, similar to that of The Emirates, which we also viewed from the train window earlier. The concourse that runs behind the lower tier seats is very spacious, with a large bar behind our chosen seats. It would be rude not to sample a pint.

The game was always going to be an uphill task for the hosts due to a sending off within the first five minutes. Bradford scored twice before MK Dons pulled one back on the stroke of half-time. During the break, Paul and I decided to see if we could walk to the side of the pitch for a different view of the game. Without any trouble we sat in some empty seats not far from the dugouts. Two more goals from the visitors killed the home atmosphere and it was only the away following you could hear, as they ran out comfortable 4-1 winners. After the game we headed into the Club Red bar for another pint. We walked into the corporate area where the Man of the Match award took place before heading downstairs to the main reception. We spoke to a gentleman in a MK Dons blazer jacket and explained our goal of a dugout photo. He escorted us down to the changing rooms area and out through the tunnel. As we were chatting in the tunnel area, Bradford City manager Stuart McCall finished his post-match interview and stopped for a photo as well. We thanked everyone for their hospitality, and set off on our return journey which consisted of a taxi, train, train, taxi, arriving home at half past midnight, with only 11 more grounds to go.

28/10/17 – The Valley
My son Scott decided he wanted a new car, and searched the internet for the exact type he wanted. He found the one he wanted in Crawley, only 340 miles and a six hour drive away. I was asked if I would drive him there so he could pick it up. I agreed on the proviso that I would drop him off and take in a match before the long drive home. Two birds, one stone. I checked for games in and around London and decided on

Wycombe Wanderers. My good friend Mr Webb contacted me and he came up trumps with the news that a pal of his, Graeme Fyvie, was linesman at Charlton Athletic that day and there would be two tickets left in my name if I wanted them. Hell yes, Wycombe can wait. I asked Paul if he was up for the trip and he readily agreed.

A very early start before the sun came up saw us on our way, arriving at the garage around 11.30am. A quick look at the car, saying goodbye to Scott, and it was back into the Clio for the hour long trip into the capital. Paul came up with the idea of using a 'Parking App' so we could get near to the ground without the risk of being clamped or towed away. He found one where he paid £6 and parked the car on someone's drive which was only a few hundred yards from the ground. We walked down the hill and arrived at The Valley around 1.30pm.

At the ground we were not only given a pair of tickets, but also two passes for the 'Players & Officials Lounge'. We made our way up the stairs and sampled the free coffee and biscuits. Paul wasn't in the mood for coffee and ordered a pint of Foster's. Sadly, for him, this wasn't complimentary and he had to stump up £4.50 for it. As we arrived slightly later than planned, we didn't manage to speak to Graeme to say thank you, but we definitely appreciated it. With an hour still to kick-off, I went for a little walkabout in the virtually empty stadium and spoke to a steward about a dugout photo. He agreed, so I ran back up the stairs like an excited child to grab Paul. I must say, I was quite impressed by The Valley. It's a decent sized 27,000 all-seater stadium. Sadly, it was less than half full for the visit of AFC Wimbledon in this League One encounter.

With the score goal-less at half time, we were praying for goals to come in the second half. Fortunately for us, and for Charlton, there was one. A free kick was smashed home but I think the visiting keeper should have done better. After the game, we headed back to the Players Lounge to let the London traffic disperse. We got chatting to a scout from Lincoln City, who travels up and down the country writing reports on players and oppositions and feeding them back. What a job that is.

We headed for home and as we were south of the River Thames the sat-nav directed towards the 'The O2 Arena' using The Blackwall Tunnel. If you have ever seen Wacky Races as a kid, then this was the real thing. There were five lanes of traffic trying to get in two lanes with mad motorbike riders squeezing through gaps which weren't there. Once we navigated that we drove past the London Stadium, West Ham's new home, and I commented that I would be back at Christmas for Newcastle's visit there.

11/11/17 – Broadfield Stadium

It was another International break for the top two divisions, and I had noticed, that there could be the possibility of a two-in-one weekend starting at Crawley Town. Paul had to abstain from this trip due to a previous engagement, but another mate of mine, Mackem Adam said he was up for it. Adam is also a South Shields fan and due to Sunderland's shit state of affairs, has turned his back on his dying club. Another fella who was up for the trip was Pete, a Southampton and Yeovil Town supporter who lives in Nottingham.... don't ask!! He is the creator of the website 'www.the92.net' where crazy people such as me, can record trips to all grounds across the country in their quest. I met him last Easter when we went to St. James Park and the Stadium of Shite on consecutive days.

Adam and I set off in the trusty Clio and arranged to collect Pete just off the M1. We had booked a room at a hotel which was walking distance from Crawley's tiny ground. We dropped the car off, got checked in and headed for food and beer. We made our way to the ground, and easily secured our dugout photo, before sampling the beer in the bar attached to the ground. If you ever fancy going to Crawley, I suggest you drink bottles. The pints we were served were as flat as a witches tit.

Just over 2,000 fans saw Crawley and Forest Green Rovers play out a 1-1 draw in League Two. Once again it was scoreless at half time, but the visitors took the lead just after the hour mark. This lead lasted for about ten minutes before Crawley took a share of the spoils. This was my 100th league ground that I have visited, but number 83 of the current 92, and I have to say, The Checkatrade.com Stadium was probably the worst.

After the game, we headed back to the hotel for a quick shower, then out for a curry. The curry was excellent, and the pub next to the hotel was open till 1am where we stayed till we got kicked out. Back to the digs to get our head down ready for another huge game the following day.

12/11/17 – *Kingsmeadow*

We were up nice and early for an hour's drive up to see AFC Wimbledon take on Peterborough in League One. We found some cafe next to the ground called 'Fat Boys' so we knew this would be ideal for our breakfast. Three huge plates were quickly devoured before walking to the ground which is shared with the Chelsea Ladies Football team.

My mate David Webb had sent an email to today's referee Darren Handley, like he did for the Barnet game, but once again he never replied. Therefore we didn't get complimentary tickets meaning we all had pay £20 to stand along the side of the pitch. We were allowed in for a dugout photo, and as we were walking around the pitch Adam stepped onto the pitch by about six inches, and a scream from the groundsman informed us, in no uncertain terms, we were not allowed on it. After the photos we were escorted back down the tunnel, and we walked past the match officials. I introduced myself to Mr Handley as a friend of David's and explained the issue about him not replying to his email. He explained he had changed email address and would contact my good friend later that evening and promised he would help if he could for any future games he had. We headed for the bar and this is where the club's small trophy cabinet is housed. Inside the cabinet was a picture of Vinny Jones celebrating his FA Cup triumph with Wimbledon (not the MK Dons) as well as his medal from that day in 1988.

We stood on the terrace and as I looked around I realised I had been hasty in my thoughts that Crawley was the worst ground out of the 92. Sadly, this one takes top spot.

The visitors lined up with the ex-Newcastle player, that all mackems hate, Steven Taylor as well as ex-Gateshead player Marcus Maddison in their starting eleven. The Wombles took the lead within the first minute, but went behind thanks to two goals from The Posh including a penalty from Maddison. Wimbledon equalised on the stroke of half time to end a pulsating first period. The second half wasn't as entertaining and the only talking point was a bit of theatrics from Maddison, trying to con the ref into believing he had been head-butted, when two players squared up to each other. They both got a yellow card, and Maddison should be ashamed of himself, quite embarrassing.

The long drive back home, via Nottingham, capped off a great weekend for the three of us.

21/11/17 – Bescot Stadium

The Walsall v Fleetwood Town game was hastily chosen. I don't normally do midweek games, unless it involves Newcastle, but a call from David Webb to say Darren Handley had been in touch with the offer of referee's guest tickets, made our minds up quite easily. Paul and I both had a day's holiday granted and off we went.

We arrived quite early, before the referee in fact, and just hung around outside the ground visiting the club shop etc. We asked at reception for the tickets but they hadn't been processed yet, so instead asked for a dugout photo. This was not a problem as soon as I mentioned we were guests of the referee. We saw Mr Handley arrive from his car, and surprisingly he remembered me from Wimbledon and said he would sort the tickets. He then sent us upstairs to the corporate area where he would meet us once he had dropped of his kit at the changing rooms. When we got to the 'Officials Area' the table was set up with a spread of sandwiches, coffee and biscuits. We just sat there, not wanting to munch on them before anyone else appeared. The referee then appeared, as did his assistants and fourth official as well as a couple of their guests, and we all chatted away before the game. Then, a face I recognised pulled up a chair and joined in chatting. It was the ex-Premier League referee Phil Dowd. Phil was great. Once he found out we were Newcastle fans he was talking about the times he sent off Joey Barton and Shola Ameobi. He also informed us on the fact he was referee for the remarkable 4-4 draw against Arsenal where Cheick Tiote (Rest in Peace) scored that great volley.

The Banks' Stadium, as it is known as, is a decent ground with an impressive stand behind one goal. The other three stands are very adequate for this level. The visitors, managed by Uwe Rosler, took the lead but Walsall hit back twice to lead at half time. Fleetwood grabbed an equaliser and this is how the score stayed until the last minute. Walsall scored two more within a minute to snatch the three points with a 4-2 win. I'm sure a few of the 3,000 crowd missed those goals by leaving early.

We stayed near the reception after the game in order to thank the referee for his hospitality. He even offered us tickets for his next game at Carlisle on the Saturday. Sadly, I had to decline his offer as Newcastle were playing at home that day.

2/12/17 – The New Den

I had planned another two-in-one weekend for the beginning of December, as travelling as far as I had to made perfect sense. I knew that a visit to the notorious Millwall would have to take place sooner or later so I asked Paul if he was up for it. Once he agreed I booked a hotel outside of London so we could travel straight there after this game, and be closer to our venue for the Sunday game. The drive south was easy enough but as soon as you reached the centre of London it was a nightmare. We drove through Tavistock Square and Russell Square, where the tragic '7/7 Bombings' took place in 2005, before crossing the River Thames via Waterloo Bridge. We deliberately arrived at Millwall well before noon so that we could watch the early kick-off, which was Newcastle away at Chelsea, in a bar somewhere near. As there weren't many people about, we headed for reception and were allowed in for a dugout photo. From there we headed for some lunch at The Millwall Cafe right outside the ground.

85

When we asked about any local pubs, we were told to walk around to the back of the Cold Blow Lane Stand, where the doors are open for fans to have a drink and watch the televised match on the screens. Now, I thought Millwall fans hated everyone, including their mothers, so I thought watching this game should be ok. The first young kid to walk in holding his Dad's hand soon answered my question. 'C'mon Chelsea', he shouted at the screen. We decided to keep quiet for the duration of the game. Sadly, Newcastle lost 3-1 despite taking an early lead, and we headed for the ticket office.

We were to be sat one row from the back of the Main stand, with the away followers of Sheffield United behind the goal to our left, and the nutters of Millwall behind the goal to our right. The atmosphere was quite hostile with the chorus of 'Let 'em Come Down to the Den' welcoming the players onto the pitch. This was swiftly followed by the 'No-one likes us, we don't care' chant. We were sat directly behind a set of geezers, all in the late forties, early fifties wearing flat caps and designer gear. The match was less than a minute old when the first foul saw a home player take a tumble. 'You dirty northern kant!!' screamed the head geezer followed by a few of his pals quickly joining in. Considering Paul and I were from well over 100 miles further north than Sheffield, we kept our voices low.

Ex-Newcastle player Shane Ferguson was in the starting line up for Millwall, and he was doing his best to get up and down the left wing. Millwall opened the scoring but were pegged back just before half-time in a fairly even encounter. However, two second half goals from the hosts meant that the locals went home happy with a 3-1 win. We walked back to the car and headed for our hotel. We hit the town for food and a few beers, and we found out the great news that Paul had become a Granddad for the first time.

3/12/17 – Adams Park

After our overnight stay in High Wycombe, this meant a short trip in the morning to see Wycombe Wanderers v Leatherhead in the FA Cup Round Two. We parked in the nearby Industrial estate which would make for a quick getaway after the final whistle. Once again, we ventured in to reception, explained what we were doing and asked for a dugout photo. Better was to come when a match day host took us into the home dressing room for a look around, down the tunnel and into the dugouts. This is what I like about smaller clubs; most are so friendly and are not just interested in getting every last penny out of you.

As we sat down for the start of the game, I noticed to my right was ex-toon centre forward Mick Harford, on scouting duty for Luton Town. Even though he is a mackem I asked him for a, photo and he duly obliged.

Non-league side Leatherhead had brought a decent 1000-strong following and they made some noise with the total attendance being just under 4,000. The away fans erupted after only eight minutes, when they scored from a penalty and dreamed of a giant-killing. It was not to be though as three Wycombe goals, including a stoppage time diving header from Ade Akinfenwa sealed their place in the hat for round three.

20/1/18 – London Stadium

I was supposed to be ticking this ground off just before Christmas when Newcastle were playing here. However, my better half decided to book a holiday in Fuerteventura meaning I wasn't able to go. Newcastle were playing away at Manchester City in the evening kick-off so we decided on a train trip this time round. Paul and Adam decided to come along, and another pal of mine Chris Pearson, managed to get me half price train tickets thanks to his lovely girlfriend. The price of tickets for a home fan ranged from £55 upwards, so as West Ham were playing Bournemouth, I become a Cherries fan in order to buy three tickets in the away end capped at £30 each.

From Kings Cross, we headed to Stratford International, then onto the huge Westfield Shopping centre where we demolished a KFC. A pub right next to the stadium were charging well over £5 a pint, so we only had one before heading to look around this former Olympic venue. The heavens opened so we darted inside for shelter and more overly-priced beer. The stadium is lovely. It's just not a football stadium. It was virtually a sell-out however there was no atmosphere from the home fans, or the away fans for that matter. The game was a typical Premier League game where both sides are happy to make the numbers up in the league and are desperate not to lose.

The game came to life with twenty minutes left. Bournemouth opened the scoring, but conceded straight from the restart. A pulsating 60 seconds woke the crowd, but they soon fell back asleep.

The game ended 1-1, and the fun of getting out was just about to start. Stewards were lined up like riot police with workmen's Stop/Go signs trying to control the flow of 57,000 fans trying to get home. We eventually got back to Kings Cross, bought some cans from the shop, and stood in the largest McDonald's queue I've ever seen. Fortunately we made it onto the train with two minutes to spare!

3/2/18 – Huish Park

A 370 miles trip to Yeovil Town v Cambridge United in League Two sounds mad. Because of this, I requested an overnight stay which was granted by my lovely, caring and very understanding wife. Paul and Adam's beloveds also agreed.

Setting off in the dark early hours meant a six-hour plus journey, arriving at the hotel in enough time to drop our bags and get a taxi for the short ride to the ground. We headed to reception; dugout photo completed, then took in a look around the club shop. Tickets to stand behind the goal for £17 each were purchased. Adam tried to haggle with the sales assistant, bartering for a discount for a scarf, to which he was given 20% off. A few pints in the marquee before kick-off were lovingly sampled. The game was goal-less at half-time which meant a swift one back at the marquee, returning just in time for the restart. Paul didn't make the kick-off as his weak bladder was causing him problems, but he returned just as Yeovil had a free kick in a promising position. The ball whistled past the post and hit the part of the terrace where Paul was stood. It missed him by millimetres, and I'm sure if it had connected he would have been visiting Yeovil Royal hospital for the night. Two goals for the home side meant most of the 2,500 in attendance went home happy.

As it was a pleasant evening we decided to walk the two miles back to the hotel stopping off at a pub on the way. By now, the five pints before and during the game had taken affect on Paul, because this usually quiet guy started to abuse a local gentleman for drinking white wine. We headed back to the hotel and arranged for us to sample a local curry house. Paul ordered a lamb shank, and Adam and I had a Ruby Murray. Paul hardly touched his so after we had finished ours, we helped him with his. The next part of the plan was to go to the local Wetherspoons, but Paul had taken in all he could. He was packed into a taxi while we headed for the bar.

Two pint cocktail pitchers of Mojito and Long Island Iced Tea were ordered and when it was each other's round we just bought double Bacardi and double Jack Daniels to give the cocktails some kick. Adam went outside for a smoke and some random bloke asked him for a kiss. He must have been impressed with the way Adam was sucking on his cocktail's straw! He quickly got the message when he was told politely where to go.

We got back to the hotel around midnight where we knocked Paul out of bed. As he got up, he got his foot caught in the duvet and went arse-over-tit.

We woke in the morning feeling rather fresh. We all tucked into our breakfasts before starting another six hour journey home.

17/3/18 – Whaddon Road

The final International break of the season allowed me to complete a 500 mile round trip to see Cheltenham Town v Chesterfield in League Two. Once again, the three stooges of Paul, Adam and I jumped into the old Clio and off we went.

We had planned on visiting this ground two weeks earlier; however the game was postponed due to 'The Beast From The East' dumping a load of snow across the country. The temperatures around the place were just above freezing when we arrived, so we headed to the ground for a quick dugout photo, before feeling warmth in the bar in the main stand.

As we were inside the bar, there was a collection to raise money for the Mayor's charity and as she walked by I dropped a quid into her bucket and asked for a photo. Moments later, some other bloke came past shaking his bucket, to which I told him that his boss has just been around. A Cheltenham Town fan sitting on the table next to us then informed me that he was actually the football club's chairman!

We braved the cold and stood on the terrace in front of the main stand which runs alongside the pitch, and as per usual there were no goals in the first half. Chesterfield were in a relegation spot and gave themselves a glimmer of hope when they scored with 15 minutes remaining. Cheltenham threw on their last substitute and within a minute, he had scored with his first touch of the ball to equalise.

With the game over we, along with the 2,800 other hardly souls in attendance, headed for warmth. Ours was to be the heaters of the car on full blast as we headed north. We got as far as Doncaster when the road signs said road closed due to an accident. With nowhere to go, we sat in the car for 45 minutes as the snow once again started to fall around us. At last, we were back on the move, albeit quite slowly due to the snow, and got home close to 1am.

30/3/18 – Community Stadium

My penultimate ground was Colchester United's relatively new stadium, for their League Two match against promotion chasing Luton Town, on Good Friday. Paul couldn't make this trip, but Adam came along. My mate Pete from Nottingham was joining us there as he was ticking off his own two-in-one weekend, having watched a game the night before. We picked him up from his hotel which was a couple of miles from the ground. Coincidentally, he was staying at the same hotel as the Luton Town side, and managed to get a photo with the manager Nathan Jones. He, as Pete informed me, is an ex-Yeovil player.

Colchester's pricing policy is an odd one. Our tickets were for the home stand behind the goal, but the earlier you bought the ticket, the cheaper it was. The price started at £14 when they first went on sale, going up to £21 if bought on the day. I got ours 10 days in advance and paid £17.50 for them. We arrived early and headed for reception. We were escorted pitchside for our dugout photo and shown to where the press were gathering. Just as we were leaving, the away team bus arrived and the players all walked past us. Nathan Jones must have thought Pete was stalking him as he said hello to him again.

Outside the ground, there was a band playing some decent stuff. They were oddly called 'The Four Man Trio' and blasted out classics from The Jam, The Undertones, Oasis et al. However, the rain came so the atmosphere was somewhat dampened.

The game itself was less than minute old when a horrific injury to Luton's Luke Berry saw the ref take the players off the field for a twelve minute delay. The rain kept coming and the water was causing some puddles on the pitch. It was a long way to come for an abandoned game. The delay, and injury, seemed to affect the Luton players and Colchester took advantage scoring from some sloppy defending. They home side doubled their lead to go in with a comfortable half time lead. The second half saw Luton pile on the pressure, but with the rain still falling they couldn't get through a resilient defence. They did pull one back through a Danny Hylton penalty in the 88th minute but the points stayed in Colchester.

The journey home was to be via Nottingham, and let's just say it was interesting. First of all, there was a fire at Stansted Airport which meant all the flights were cancelled. This meant miles of traffic at a standstill but it didn't cause us too much problems. Following this was the moment I thought I wouldn't make it to number 92. I was travelling in the outside lane, doing around 80mph. It was drizzling with still a bit of surface water, when the lorry in the inside lane started to drift into my lane. I slammed on the brakes and readied myself for impact. Adam, in the front seat lifted his legs up to avoid injury, and Pete in the back gripped onto the seat in front of him. Amazingly, my trusty 13-year old Clio went from 80mph to zero in enough time to stop less than a foot from the back of the lorry. With my heart beating through my chest, we headed for the nearest services for a well-earned coffee and a visit to the toilet to change my pants!! The rest of the journey was taken at a lower speed but still we were hitting patches of water on the motorway which kept me alert. Arriving home after midnight, it was good to be home.

21/4/18 – St James Park (Number 92)

The day had arrived for me to complete my tour of The 92 grounds. From my first ever match as a schoolboy, watching my beloved Newcastle United at St James Park to the other St James Park, Exeter. It wasn't my 92nd league ground though but my 106th in total.

One night in our local, we were discussing the journey, to which my mate David said he would drive us all to Exeter in his mini bus. We hastily agreed, and even decided to bring our wives along for the trip. The ladies would spend the day shopping and drinking while we went to the match. David's geography isn't his strong point and it was a few days later when he realised how far away it actually is.

On the Saturday morning the 4am alarm clock sounded and Paul, Adam, David and I, as well as our respective wives, jumped in David's mini bus for our 6 hour plus journey south, totalling 360 miles. We arrived at the hotel around 11am, got checked in, said our goodbyes to the wives and headed for the ground, stopping at some local watering hole on the way. The weather was glorious, with the temperatures in the low 20's. We arrived at 'the other' St James Park around 1pm for a pre-arranged dugout photo. I'd emailed Exeter City to inform them of my attendance completing the 92, and they readily agreed to show me pitchside. When we got pitchside, the club photographer and social media manager were also there, and escorted the four of us out onto the pitch into the centre circle for another photo. This was then posted on Exeter City's official Twitter page. The ground is under-going a major redevelopment, and as such is only made up of two stands. The main stand is all seated, and the Big Bank standing terrace behind one goal. The Big Bank is the largest standing terrace in the league, and where our tickets were for. After the photos were taken we made our way back out to Red Square, where the bar areas were and sampled a couple of pints of real ale. The club also gave me a free Exeter scarf to remember the day, however I could not put it on as wearing a red & white scarf is strictly forbidden in my family...

We took our places on the Big Bank, and I must say the atmosphere was excellent. The 'Red Legion' together with their drum ensured nothing was heard from the small away following at the other end of the main stand. With promotion in sight, three points were needed today.

A silence fell on the Big Bank as Crawley took the lead, but with a few minutes left of the half the scores were level. Exeter took the lead on the hour mark and with news of promotion rivals Wycombe Wanderers losing at home, this made the noise levels go up further. However, Crawley equalised themselves and the frustration was apparent within the home supporters. The game ended 2-2 which was great for a neutral but not for the home supporters, as they knew this was two points dropped in the race for promotion.

The end of the game saw me struggling to contain my grin at my mackem mate Adam. His team Sunderland, as the app on my phone informed me, had conceded twice in the last few minutes at home to Burton Albion, which meant they were relegated to the third tier of English football. We walked back to the hotel to meet up with the ladies, before enjoying a night out in town. The night saw plenty of alcohol which leads to a discussion about how giraffes walk. This escalated into a giraffe race down Exeter High Street between David, Paul and I. Adam was a non-runner. A local Police car suddenly pulls up to ask what we were doing. Paul explains we were giraffe racing to the amazement of the police-woman in the driver seat. 'It's a common event where we are from' he adds. I walk around to the copper in the passenger seat and challenge him to a race. He swiftly refuses saying 'not in a million years' and told us to enjoy the rest of our night. We certainly did.

So the journey is over, for now. This is an ongoing project where any new stadium, or teams promoted into the league, must be visited to ensure my achievement never fades.

What or where shall I do next? Scotland, perhaps? Who knows?

..........to be continued

Epilogue
Distances
Here is a quick calculation of the approximate miles covered in a round trip from St James Park to the other stadiums.

1	Newcastle United	0
2	Leeds United	166
3	Stockport County	222
4	Nottingham Forest	284
5	Sunderland (old)	20
6	Middlesbrough (old)	64
7	Sheffield United	222
8	Barnsley	197
9	Notts County	284
10	Swindon Town	472
11	Manchester City (old)	216
12	Sheffield Wednesday	216
13	Bolton Wanderers (old)	205
14	Blackburn Rovers	186
15	Hartlepool United	51
16	Coventry City (old)	354
17	Derby County	285
18	Manchester United	216
19	Preston North End	187
20	Birmingham City	346
21	Carlisle United	103
22	Darlington (old)	63
23	Everton	239
24	Leicester City (old)	327
25	Aston Villa	342
26	Bradford City	162
27	Sunderland	20
28	Bolton Wanderers	206
29	Tottenham (old)	483
30	Southampton	563
31	West Ham United (old)	495
32	West Bromwich Albion	342

33	Leicester City	328
34	Darlington	65
35	Middlesbrough	64
36	Portsmouth	579
37	Arsenal (old)	489
38	Manchester City	211
39	Chelsea	497
40	Liverpool	239
41	Doncaster Rovers	207
42	Coventry City	349
43	Wigan Athletic	214
44	Hull City	198
45	Stoke City	278
46	Crystal Palace	510
47	Blackpool	198
48	Peterborough United	352
49	Scunthorpe United	206
50	Watford	470
51	Reading	494
52	Plymouth Argyle	668
53	Queens Park Rangers	493
54	Accrington Stanley	178
55	Wolves	332
56	Huddersfield Town	183
57	Arsenal	489
58	Stevenage	442
59	Fulham	497
60	Rotherham United (old)	219
61	Oldham Athletic	201
62	Norwich City	404
63	Brighton	583
64	Swansea City	499
65	Cardiff City	501
66	Morecambe	161
67	Gillingham	528
68	Burnley	171
69	York City	145

70	Rochdale	193
71	Mansfield Town	256
72	Fleetwood Town	185
73	AFC Bournemouth	586
74	Bury	200
75	Northampton Town	383
76	Port Vale	270
77	Southend United	511
78	Bristol City	496
79	Crewe Alexandra	269
80	Rotherham United	215
81	Grimsby Town	232
82	Chesterfield	239
83	Burton Albion	298
84	Brentford	494
85	Oxford United	452
86	Newport County	482
87	Bristol Rovers	489
88	Cambridge United	409
89	Ipswich Town	463
90	Luton Town	438
91	Shrewsbury Town	329
92	Forest Green Rovers	456
93	Lincoln City	258
94	Barnet	479
95	MK Dons	416
96	Charlton Athletic	501
97	Crawley Town	549
98	AFC Wimbledon	506
99	Walsall	334
100	Millwall	499
101	Wycombe Wanderers	467
102	West Ham United	493
103	Yeovil Town	563
104	Cheltenham Town	426
105	Colchester United	470
106	Exeter City	608

Total = 35,094 miles

Another Epilogue

The European Stadiums

11/3/03 – The San Siro
Inter Milan v Newcastle

One of the greatest trips I have ever been on. I had the pleasure
to spend two nights with eleven other lads. Six of us, Steve,
Wigs, Ray, Parker, Sheeran and I caught a flight from Newcastle
to Amsterdam and from there to Milan; while the other six,
Stansfield, Mark Reay, Stu, Hawksfield, Michael and little Kyle
went via Heathrow.

KLM were such great hosts on each flight as they gave us
complimentary drinks. We were sat across the full back row of
the plane and each time an air hostess walked past us we asked
for six more. Each time they obliged. As we were getting off, she
gave us all another to drink in the airport. Schiphol Airport is
huge. We walked about two miles from the one terminal we
landed at to the one we needed to be at to take off for Milan.
Fortunately, we had plenty of time between connecting flights
for us to sample some more local beer.

We arrived into Milan, and jumped into a six-seater taxi to take
us to the hotel. I was sitting in the middle of the back seat and all
the way from the airport the driver was staring at me through his
rear-view mirror. He hardly spoke any English but enough to get
by. The ride was crazy, not braking until the last second as
though he was in a Formula One car at Monza. We arrived at the
hotel and as we were getting our bags from the boot, the driver
gave me a drawing of me that he had done whilst driving.... That
explained why he was staring so much.

We waited at the hotel till the other six arrived around 30
minutes later. On check-in, we discovered the four of us in our
room had to be content with double beds. I shared with Steve,
while Wigs and Ray would snuggle up in the other.

We, along with a few thousand other Geordies, congregated near
to Duomo Cathedral before making our way to the match.

Sheeran got so pissed on this first afternoon that we got asked to leave one cafe. The owner was shouting at him when he came back from the toilets, so we tried to find out what the problem was. Apparently he started pissing on the stairs, long before he made it to the toilets. He even pulled his chair into the middle of the zebra crossing and sat down. Zebra crossings in Milan are not like they are at home and he soon shifted when the cars started hurtling past him.

Little Kyle had bought a small football and we started to boot it as high as we could. Everyone was in high spirits; even tourists were laughing and joining in. All of a sudden a group of policemen confiscated the ball. Little Kyle, who was 18 but actually looked 14, started pleading with the copper like a little choirboy, his hands clasped together like he was praying. He eventually got it back.

As we got near to the ground the bars were serving beer poured straight from the bottle into plastic glasses. What they didn't mention was it was non-alcoholic lager. Sheeran still managed to get pissed on it.

It was time to head to the stadium, and as we turned the corner to witness the San Siro for the first time, the hairs stood up on the back of my neck. It was huge and went up and up into the Italian night sky. We walked into the away end to see 12,000 away fans packed into the section behind the goal. We stood towards the corner flag nearest to the dugouts. The Italian fans above us were throwing everything from coins, fruit, piss and even a flare at us.

When Alan Shearer scored just before half time, the place erupted. It reminded of the scenes at Old Wembley when Rob Lee scored a header in the FA Cup semi final three years earlier. Inter equalised early in the second half, before Shearer scored again in front of us. Once again, we went mental. Inter pulled us back once more and the game ended 2-2.

The next morning, all twelve of us headed out for breakfast, and a stroll, and to sample more expensive beer. Each bar waited till you had finished drinking before telling you how much it cost. We soon got wise, and decided to send one person in to ask in true Geordie fashion 'Mucho costo bier grande?' If it was reasonable, we would then order a dozen!!

We sat outside a cafe drinking in the sunshine when a couple of smart young Italian girls walked by. A few typical remarks and whistles followed, to which the girls responded by flicking their hair, smiling and glancing back at us. As one of them was looking at us she didn't notice the bollard in the pathway and walked straight into it. They didn't hang around much longer as we were howling with laughter.

We ended up visiting the Armani store which was a very peaceful shop covering three floors. There was a security bloke on the door that was straight on his radio as soon as we walked in. Wigs acknowledged him with an 'Alreet bonny lad?' We all seemed to walk in different directions, but breaking the silence every few minutes were loud comments such as 'you got these in a 36, pet?' or my very own exclamation 'fucking how much for a tie?'

Later that afternoon, we were in a bar when the bar staff started preparing a huge display of foods. It took her about 45 minutes to set up and it was a very well presented array of meats, cheeses and salads. Curiosity got the better of me, so I shouted 'Is this all gratis, for us?' The barman nodded, and the twelve of us destroyed it in about a minute. A few locals pecked at what we had left, like a group of hungry pigeons but it was slim pickings. Wigs was disappointed when he asked for more spicy sausage and they turned him down.

That night we hit the town, but somehow Stansfield, Ray and I got separated from the group and ended up in the bar from earlier. The looks on the locals' faces were a picture when the DJ played Jump Around by House of Pain and the three of us went mental on the tiny dance floor.

Our final day saw us stumble across a shoe shop by the name of 'Cocks'. It was an obvious photo opportunity for the group. A tourist took the photo then asked Mark Reay if he would return the favour and take a photograph of him and his wife. Mark proceeded to get hold of his camera then ran off into the distance. We all fell about laughing as the tourist looked on in amazement and stunned silence.

25/3/04 – Estadio Son Moix
Real Mallorca v Newcastle
The UEFA Cup draw gave us an opportunity to take a trip to
Majorca. Eugene and I decided it would be great and looked for
a cheap trip. Sadly, the only cheap trip we could find involved a
week-long all inclusive holiday with a flight from Gatwick. We
drove through the night on the Sunday evening ready for our
Monday morning flight. In the departure lounge at 4am we
ordered our first pints of the trip.

The weather wasn't great that week so we made do with a
drinking trip. We found a bar that claimed to be the Balearics
branch of the Manchester City Supporters Club. This was to be
our base for the week.

I had never really seen racism up close and this trip opened my
eyes. I was amazed at how bad some of the Spanish people were.
Maybe they didn't know they were doing it, and it certainly didn't
bother Eugene. Simple things such as when he was waiting to be
served at the bar. The bar staff would serve others before him
even though he'd been stood there a while. Also quite odd were
the strange looks we got, as a white man and a black man were
walking along the beach front chatting to each other. Someone
asked us how we become friends and Eugene said 'I'm back and
he's white. We are Newcastle United'. We were sitting in a
Karaoke bar and discussed singing Ebony and Ivory, but decided
against it.

The match was on the Thursday so we made our way from
where we were staying in Can Pastilla the ten miles to Palma. We
were in a bar when a lad started chatting to us. He was a
Newcastle fan, who now lives in Spain as a journalist. He spoke
excellent Spanish so we took him under our wing to act as our
guide and interpreter. It worked exceptionally well as the taxi
drivers knew exactly where we wanted to go and the local police
instructed us where to find a bar afterwards that would serve us.
We got to the ground with the rain falling on about 3,000
alcohol fuelled Geordies. The tickets had a barcode system to
allow supporters access. Due to the rain our tickets had become
wet and we struggled to scan them. Eventually mine worked but

no such joy for Eugene. Typically, the huge police presence saw this particular 'Policia Local' grab Eugene's ticket from his hand, gave it the once-over, and tore it in half. I thought he wasn't going to get in, but the annoyed copper then pushed him through. Another bit of racism, perhaps? I thought so. There weren't many locals inside the ground due to the fact the first leg had seen Newcastle win 4-1.

The first half was goalless as Newcastle attacked the goal we were stood behind. Three second half goals came, to see the toon comfortable winners. There was also a debut for Steven Taylor, who at the end made a bee-line for Samuel Eto'o in order to grab a souvenir shirt.

On the Saturday, with our flight home still two nights away, we decided on an all-night drinking session till the sun came up. We found a bar that promised to stay open as long as we were drinking. The bar had a range of mini games which we drunkenly played throughout the marathon. There was mini pool, mini darts, mini table tennis and mini bar-football. Even better were the cheap bottles of Budweiser. Every time we bought two bottles we were given a scratch card. As they were printed in Spanish we had no idea what we had won. On the first few occasions, we were told it was a key-ring. Our suspicions were aroused when we were given another key-ring even though the words on the scratch card weren't the same as before. It was around 5am when I collected up all twelve or so key-rings, and walked behind the bar to rummage in the Bud box from where they had come from. I dropped them all back in and removed two hoodies with the Budweiser logo on them. I gave one to Eugene and I put the other one on. The young girl was pleading with us for them back but we refused. We finished our drinks and headed for our hotel bed. We woke up well after lunch and made our way to the all inclusive restaurant, only to be told it was closed. We checked our watches and demanded to know why. Nobody told us that they put the clocks forward in Majorca as well!!!

We found a restaurant that served the usual full English breakfast before deciding on a walk round to the bar from last night. As soon as we walked in the owner asked if we were the two lads who took the hoodies last night, to which we denied all knowledge. His reply was simple but great, 'well lads, you certainly match the description...'

17/4/05 – Millennium Stadium
Manchester United v Newcastle

This game came not long after the trip to Man City's new stadium, so we asked Paul Piggford if he fancied being our minibus driver again. He agreed and as there were only six of us going he brought his son along for the ride. The usual crew of Wigs, Parker, Stu, Sheeran, Mick and I were picked from the car park of Asda Gateshead at midnight in order to drive the seven hours or so to Cardiff. This gave us plenty of time to find a pub which served breakfast, as well as early beers. It also gave the driver plenty of time to get some sleep ready for the long drive home.

The stadium looked excellent but even though the heavens opened, the retractable roof didn't close and the pitch got well watered, similar to the Geordie fans.

The game itself was fairly one-sided and ManUre deserved their two goal half time lead. It was three not long after the restart but Newcastle scored almost straight from kick off through Shola Ameobi. It was a just reward for the great following showed by the fans. The game was over when Cristiano Ronaldo scored and the lads trundled off the pitch to a warm applause. Applause for each player except Nicky Butt though; as he made his way off the pitch with all the Man Utd players smiling away and generally not bothered about those in the black and white.

28/4/07 – Mini Estadi
Barcelona B v Valencia B

On our way back from collecting our tickets for the following day's game at the Nou Camp, Scott and I walked past the smaller stadium near to the ground and could hear a game taking place.

We tried to get in but each turnstile was closed. We spotted a steward and started to question him about what was going on. He said it was the reserve side playing, but we needed to buy a ticket if we wanted to go in. I said I had tickets for tomorrow's game and those seemed to be the magic words. He immediately opened a gate and allowed us in. The game had just about five minutes of the first half remaining so we stayed till the end to see the game finish 2-2. There was a young 16 year old lad playing for Barcelona who the locals were raving about. He went by the name of Bojan.

He definitely had some skill and pace about him, but I wondered if he could do it on a cold Tuesday night in Stoke.....

29/4/07 – Camp Nou
Barcelona v Levante

This trip was set up as part of Scott's 17th birthday present, and I must say what a trip it was. We had done the stadium tour a couple of days earlier and was amazed at its size. The atmosphere inside the ground was very much like a carnival, with the sun shining and fans smiling. It would be interesting to see what percentage of foreign people made up part of the 74,000 attendance. I was sat near Germans, French, Japanese, as well as a few Spanish, in the lower tier near to the corner flag opposite the dugouts. The names of the Barcelona starting eleven players roll off the tongue like a Dream Team selection. Valdes, Van Bronckhorst, Thuram, Puyol, Zambrotta, Deco, Xavi, Iniesta, Ronaldinho, Eto'o, Messi.

Barca won 1-0 thanks to a goal from Samuel Eto'o, who celebrated at the corner flag just where we were sitting. However the star of the show was undoubtedly Ronaldinho. His range of skills was immense. His 'Man of the Match' performance was closely followed by the one by Lionel Messi. I'm quite humbled and delighted to say I've seen them both play live.

7/8/10 – Ibrox
Rangers v Newcastle

A pre season friendly north of the border was announced and the train tickets were snapped up very quickly. Jonny, Bish, Stansfield and I were booked onto the quiet coach, yeah right! We got to Glasgow fairly early and decided to visit Celtic Park to see if we could blag a look about. The stewards were in a shit mood and told us we would need to pay for a stadium tour to see inside. Bollocks to that so we walked till we couldn't walk anymore and flagged a taxi down to take us across the city.

We found a pub near the ground which was quite friendly and headed for the bar. When I ordered the round in I noticed a beer on draught which was 9% alcohol by volume. I ordered a pint of that as well but the barman said he would only sell it in halves. I sampled it first, and it was fucking awful. It was like drinking marmite with the taste of cold tar. I passed the half pint to the other three lads who couldn't down anything more than a sip, before giving the rest to an 'old jakie' stood near us. He drank it like water, finished it off in one and ended it with a large grin on his face.

A 30,000 crowd saw a decent game, but Rangers went two up in the second half. The biggest cheer of the day was saved for the Newcastle substitute Peter Lovenkrands, who is a Rangers legend. With virtually his first touch of the ball he pulled a goal back for the toon, and that was as good as it got.

We piled out of Ibrox and headed down Paisley Road asking the locals for the whereabouts of a nearby pub. This fella pointed at a boarded up building with no windows and said 'that's one there'. We built up the courage and walked in. Yes, it was one of those moments when the chatter stops, every head turns to look at you and even the pool balls seemed to stop moving. Four pints ordered, four pints swiftly consumed and four blokes quickly making for the door. We grabbed some cans of Tenants Lager for the train and enjoyed a rather noisy trip south.

8/11/12 – Jan Breydel Stadium
Bruges v Newcastle
My first Newcastle European away trip in eight years was a
belter. Jonny arranged the travel and I arranged the hotel. The
travel itinerary went something like this. 4.25am train from
Newcastle to Kings Cross, tube across London to some random
station to jump in a minibus to take us to Dover. Ferry to Calais
then minibus to Bruges.
On the bus were Me, Jonny, Ridley, Gary, Chris, Carling, Darren,
Alex, Anthony, Warren and Panda, however tickets were hard to
come by and only six managed to get to the game. We were all
pissed and tired so Darren decided to wake everyone on the bus
by setting off a firecracker. The loud bangs certainly did the
trick, and kept the driver alert to.
The hotel I booked was one of the nicest places I've ever slept
in. It was a top-notch five star swanky place. Three double
rooms and a triple room for Me, Rids and Chris. On the way
there Jonny had been contacted by a random bloke who was
travelling alone, and had nowhere to stay so he arranged to tag
along with us. His name was Lee, so we called him Random Lee.
When he described himself of what we should be looking for at
the arranged meeting bar, he said 'dark hair, red top, blue jeans'.
What he failed to mention but surely would have made it easier
for us, was that he only had one eye!!!
We made our way to 'The Square' where approximately 6,000
Geordies had gathered to drink the city dry. However there were
less than 3,000 tickets for away fans so about half of the fans
stayed in the square all day, and night. Only six out of our group
had tickets and after a few beers we headed to the ground. The
local police had positioned themselves on route to guide us just
over three miles to the ground. Every now and then there would
be a checkpoint of ticket searches. If you didn't have one, you
were turned back. No taxis or buses were allowed near the
stadium, so it was a case of walking for an hour to get there, with
the same journey back to look forward to.
On arrival at the ground, Jonny and I were separated from the
other four. We were in the upper tier while Rids, Gary, Chris and

Darren were in the lower tier, right behind the goal. That goal was where the Belgian side scored twice to go two up, but before half time we were level. Vernon Anita scored a great volley, then a couple of minutes later Shola was on hand to stab in the equaliser to send the away fans wild. There was no further action and a draw was probably a fair result. The main talking point was that the attendance was 18,000 in a 29,000 capacity stadium. The fact of the matter was the 3,000 without tickets could quite easily have been accommodated.

After been kept back in the ground for twenty minutes, we made the slow walk back to meet up with the lads in a bar they had found away from the main area. We stayed there till the early hours before heading back to the hotel. Our triple room had a king-size double bed which Rids and I agreed to share, with Chris sleeping in a bed upstairs. Yes, our room was so big it had an upstairs. When we woke up in the morning, we discovered Chris had crept downstairs and climbed in our bed, because one-eyed Random Lee had climbed into his.

We headed home for the return journey, stopping off at a duty-free shop on the Belgium-France border. I bought a case of red wine, while loads of other cheap spirits were also purchased. There were also 60 cans of Jupiler Lager, a local brew of 5.2% gathered for the bus journey. Not surprisingly these didn't make it to Calais, consumed well before that.

As we had travelled from England to France, then into Belgium, then back from Belgium into France, the first time I was asked for my passport was at Calais, when we were waiting to catch our ferry to Dover. The minibus was ushered into a lane where posters warned us about not taking things such as knives, guns or animals into England. The custom officers were having a glance at our passports, and asked are you carrying anything on the bus that we shouldn't be. Anthony shouted from the back, 'just guns, puppies and kittens!' She wasn't amused and ordered all eleven off the bus. She made us get all of our bags etc and go through the scanner while she searched the bus. Strangely there were no kittens, guns or puppies found.

The bus dropped us off at the same tube station it had collected us from, and we headed for Kings Cross. The train journey was going great till Jonny stole a bottle of my red wine and passed it around the remaining nine lads. It didn't last very long, so the second bottle was opened, then the third, fourth and fifth. I held onto the sole surviving bottle, as I knew I needed something to show from this fantastic trip.

6/12/12 – Stade Chaban-Delmas
Bordeaux v Newcastle

This trip was negotiated by the way of a sweetener which involved Eugene and I taking our wives away for a three day break just before Christmas. Our journey was mammoth. A three hour train ride to London, a three hour train to Paris, and another three hour train to Bordeaux.
Newcastle had already qualified from the group stage, along with Bordeaux, so we knew this game was not going to be high on the agenda for Alan Pardew regarding his team selection. How right we were. The side was made up of reserves such as Tavernier, Marveaux, Bigirimana, Ferguson and Abeid as well as the waste of space known as Nile Ranger. Eugene and I braved the cold with approximately 1,200 other mad Geordies, including Jonny who we met up with before the game. The attendance was just short of 20,000 with the home fans behind the goal making a fair bit of noise. The game was as expected, and Newcastle lost 2-0 to a goal in each half.
We met back up with the ladies and enjoyed a couple more nights in this lovely city. We stocked up on wine and this made the nine hour journey home much more bearable.

21/2/13 – Metalist Stadium
Metalist Kharkiv v Newcastle

When the draw was made and Newcastle were faced with a trip to Ukraine, there were plenty of people up for it. However, as the time came closer the names started to drop off the list and I

108

was the only one wanting to go. About three weeks before the game, my mate Singe asked if I was still going, to which I said I didn't have anyone to go with. 'I'll go' he said, and like an excited schoolboy I quickly got to work on booking us up.

We arrived at Newcastle airport at about 5am on the Wednesday morning, and met up with some NUFC representatives who had our match tickets. They arranged the flights, hotel stay and transfers in a complete package, for £400. A four hour flight added to a two hour time difference meant we landed around 2pm local time. The place was cold, with snow covering parts of the bleak landscape. I checked the date on my phone as I thought we had landed in 1970's Russia. Everyone was wearing those Cossack hats, with long overcoats. Lada cars were everywhere, and the buildings all looked grey.

We checked into our rather nice hotel, it was not what I was expecting, and then headed off to attempt to change some money into the Ukrainian Hryvnia. 100 of these was approx £3. When we went into the exchange we had to fill out loads of forms, and hand over our passports for inspection. Every note we handed over was carefully scrutinised by the cashier before she gave us a wad of notes.

We found out quickly that not many locals speak English in these parts, and sign language is the only way to order beer. We found this bar which looked like a bunker and headed inside. There were a few other Newcastle fans from our hotel and we sat near to those. A huge 6ft 4in Ukrainian lad; about 24 years old with hands like shovels, asked us if we wanted a fight, ten on ten. I kindly declined his offer. He then asked if I had any friends who would want a fight. Again, I said no. Apparently, all fights are pre-arranged in Kharkiv and he assured me we would not be attacked while we were there... unless we carried a flag. That is seen as a challenge for them to take it from us. They then turn the flag upside down, and post photos on their Ultras website. I worked out it was one of the Ukrainians birthdays so I raised a glass and made a toast to his day. This lightened the mood somewhat.

In our hotel briefing of what to do and what not to do, the reps said don't stay out after dark. What he didn't say was in Ukraine all the street lights get switched off at 1am to save energy. Now, this happened as we were walking from the bar looking for our hotel. The place was in complete darkness. We could hear dogs barking and voices in the distance but we couldn't see ten yards in front of us. In all my years on this planet, I think this was the most frightened I've ever been. The only lights we could see were the traffic lights on a main road. We headed for this road when Singe spotted the bank from earlier where we exchanged our cash. Eventually we arrived back at the hotel and found the bar was rammed full of Geordies.

We asked for a menu as food out on the town was impossible to order. We decided on two steaks and had a few more beers. The steaks were quite some size, placed in the middle of a dinner plate. When we didn't immediately start to eat, the waiter said 'Problem?' I replied with 'Does it come with vegetables, or salad, or chips?' His response was, 'No, just meat!'

On the morning of the match, we decided to take the underground train up to the stadium for a look around. We had been warned not to travel to the match using the underground but during the day we would be fine. We got some interesting stares from the other passengers when they heard our English voices, though. After a walk around the ground and a look in the club shop, we headed back to the underground towards the city centre. Last night's steak was playing havoc with Singe's stomach so he made for the public toilet in the underground. You had to pay to use it so we found a few worthless coins from our change and gave them to the attendant. I was stood outside when after a few minutes he came out and said 'Let's go, quickly!' I thought he must have had an altercation with some local Ultras but no, it turned out he had shit everywhere. There was no toilet to sit on, just a hole in the ground. His aim wasn't too great and it ended up across the back wall of the cubicle.

Before heading to the hotel, we went for some food. We found a place which sold pizzas and cocktails. We had worked out how much Ukrainian money we had left, and how much we would need for the match, and ordered accordingly. Once the food and drink were quickly demolished, we paid the bill with all of our crumpled up notes and walked out, only to be followed out by a waitress who said we had not left enough cash. When we asked how much we were short, she said 2 Hryvnia. I started to laugh as this worked out at 6p. Singe pulled out a 20, and told her to keep the change.

We were told to be at the hotel for our bus transfer to the stadium at an agreed time, and were taken straight there under police escort. As we got off the bus we were met by lines and lines of military riot police, and searched on three separate occasions before entering. A strange rule in Kharkiv was no coins were allowed in the stadium, and if any were discovered they were soon confiscated. The match kicked off at 8pm local time, so it was 6pm back in the UK. It was around freezing point at kick off, but it was -6 degrees Celsius when the full time whistle blew.

The stadium is quite impressive, and this game was watched by an almost sold out capacity of 40,000. There were approx 500 hardy souls from Newcastle there. A full section of the home fans behind the goal to our left, removed their shirts for most of the second half when the temperatures were well below zero. I was well wrapped up with a large coat and woolly hat on, and I was staying that way, as well.

The first leg at St James' Park ended goalless as did the first half of this game. The second half saw Sissoko take a tumble in the area following a challenge from the keeper, and up stepped Shola Ameobi to smash the ball home to send Newcastle through to the next round.

We were kept in the ground for 30 minutes till the Ultras had eventually dispersed. They seemed to be heading our way at one point, until they were intercepted by a mixture of stewards and riot police. We were escorted back to the airport where our plane took off ten minutes before the team plane did, at around 1am. A few of the players in the departures lounge area chatted with the fans before heading for the VIP area. We landed back at Newcastle deep into the middle of the night, but Singe's lovely wife Nerise was there to greet us and to ensure our final part of the journey would be a lot warmer with the blowers blasting warm air into her car. My bed felt extra comfy when I finally collapsed into it.

4/4/13 – Estadio da Luz
Benfica v Newcastle

Quarter final of the UEFA Cup, and we were heading to Lisbon, Portugal. Jonny, Chris, Eugene and I all booked up to go to this one, staying for a couple of nights. A couple of days after we had booked, Singe got all of our travel details and booked a room for himself in our hotel.

The day before the game I arranged to do a stadium tour of Lisbon's other great team Sporting, with Singe and Eugene. It was very impressive and I especially like the way all the seats are made up of random colours to give the impression the stadium is full even when it's empty. On the way back I was interviewed by Portuguese TV who spotted me wearing my Newcastle shirt. We headed out for a few beers and were wandering around the side streets of Lisbon when we stopped at what looked like a butcher's shop or delicatessen. We stopped there because someone noticed they sold beer as well as meat. We even had time to sample some of the local cured ham. From there we were looking for any other random place for a drink, when I swear I saw the Benfica legend Eusebio getting out of a taxi. This is where Eugene came up with the kind of one-liner that only he could say. 'So all black men look like Eusebio do they?' We climbed a huge amount of steps to find a bar which also had Shisha Pipes on offer. I gave it a go, but it done nowt for me!! We then found a bar which sold knives. I thought this was a very strange combination. We also managed to buy five pairs of Elton John glasses for us all to wear; you can tell after a full afternoon on the drink, the alcohol had started to kick in. We ended up in a pizza shop way past midnight and I ordered some red wine. It came out in a pottery cup, not a glass. Chris, by this time was well served, and if you know him he never shuts up. He started a rendition of some Elton John song which seemed to go on forever. Luckily a taxi arrived and dropped us back at the hotel. On the day of the match, we agreed to meet up with Pyley, who was over with a few lads from our village. He told us he was in an Irish bar with a typical Irish name, such as O'Malleys or something similar. The place was full of Geordies apparently so we had to get there. We jumped in a taxi and told the driver to take us. He dropped us at an Irish Bar with the same name, but this one was empty. So we now know there are two Irish pubs in Lisbon. We simply could not do anymore to find the place we should have been so we settled for a few beers in this one. We never did see Pyley that trip.

We arrived near the stadium and it was starting to fill up. We headed into the ground for a hot dog and beer, non-alcoholic beer as we later found out. The stadium was equally as impressive as the one we visited the day before. With a few minutes to kick off, Benfica traditionally allow their mascot, an eagle, to fly around the pitch and eventually land on the arm of its trainer just as the teams walk out. I must admit it was quite a sight to behold.

Over 44,000 fans witnessed Papiss Cisse open the scoring for Newcastle at the far end of the ground, and the away section went wild. Sadly, Benfica equalized before the interval, then scored two more in the second half to run out 3-1 winners. How long will it be before we set foot onto foreign soil for our next competitive European game?

1/8/14 – Esprit Arena
Fortuna Dusseldorf v Eintracht Braunschweig

Newcastle were to play two games in the Schalke Tournament in Germany as part of their pre-season warm-up, so without the prospect of European football, it was an ideal trip away. We were staying in Dusseldorf and arrived on the Friday ready for Newcastle's games on the Saturday and Sunday. The first night was going to be just a few beers in town but a couple of lads said that Fortuna were playing at home that night in their first league game of the season, if anyone was up for it. I certainly was, so Kev Moore, Chris Thomas and I bought our tickets and headed for the stadium. The German authorities are far more advanced than their English counterparts. If you buy a match ticket, you can travel free on all public transport. That's buses, trams and trains up to two hours before and after the game. As Fortuna were in the second tier of the German League I wasn't sure what to expect. I was met with a great stadium which holds over 50,000. For this game the attendance was over 41,000. Another thing which sets them apart is the fact you can have a beer while you watch the game. Try that in England or Scotland and you end up in a cell.

We sat behind the goal in the home end with a section of away supporters behind us. At half time we strolled into the away section without any trouble and chatted with their fans. The game ended 2-2 and I was pleased I didn't pass up the chance to visit.

2/8/14 – Veltins Arena
Newcastle v Malaga

We went to Germany with Red Paul (he is called this as he once wore a red jumper), who drove to Stansted and back, as well as Jonny, and Natalie and Rebecca. I had been out celebrating my birthday that night, and got picked up at midnight for the long journey south. I climbed into the back of the car with a half-eaten pizza and a bottle of absinthe. I don't remember much about the road trip, or the flight to be honest!

When we got to the hotel we knew Jonny and I were sharing a room, however the surprise was we would also be sharing a double bed... On the first night, Jonny wasn't too impressed when I climbed in to bed naked, and he demanded boxer shorts to be worn as a minimum. There was a drunken incident in the bathroom when I squeezed one of my bollocks into a hole in the shower cubicle door (don't ask...), and Jonny was there to capture the moment on his phone. He still has that photo on his phone, and whenever I call him that's what shows up on his screen.

On the afternoon of the game we were drinking in Dusseldorf, when there were a few skirmishes between some West Ham fans and some Newcastle fans. We were all getting along nicely in the bars beforehand then something triggered the violence. Next thing we knew there were bottles thrown from bar to bar, up the street, down the street, and a few of the daft lads were going toe to toe in the square. This was quickly calmed down by the swarms of riot police which appeared out of nowhere!

We set off on the trip from Dusseldorf to Gelsenkirchen, and once again travel was free as we had match tickets. This meant two trains and a tram, plus return, as well as the ticket for the match cost us 13 Euro. We arrived at the stadium for the game, and it was a fairly low key affair with not many locals in attendance. I spotted just one bloke sporting a Malaga shirt with most of the fans being the Geordie faithful. The Schalke v West Ham game kicked off second so they hadn't started to arrive in numbers yet. Outside the ground, the sun was shining and the beer flowing. We met up with a few lads such as Beej, and also Singe and his missus. The weather was great, and eventually my t-shirt was off and my tits were out as we drank outside the stadium.

The game itself was poor, especially as Malaga raced into a three goal lead before half time. Newcastle pulled one back through Obertan but this was greeted without great celebration.

The main talking point was when a few West Ham fans nicked a Newcastle flag and tried to enter our standing section. They were quickly forced back by a few willing fight partners and a number of pints being thrown at them. Singe then said to me, 'I don't know where Nerise is. She went for beer about ten minutes ago and she hasn't come back'. With panic in both of our eyes, we stormed down to the concourse to find where she was. The commotion was still apparent and we were pushed back into stand by the riot police. Pepper spray was in the air and our eyes began to feel it. My very limited knowledge of the German language, as well as the police's limited English, resulted in us being allowed out to look for her. We spotted her outside chatting to a policewoman with two pints of lager in her hands, wondering what all the fuss was about. We all had an emotional three-way hug, and went back to watch the end of the match.

5/10/14 – Estadio da Madeira
CD Nacional v Rio Ave.

Jackie and I were on holiday in Madeira, and I noticed that there was a game on nearby while we were there. I persuaded my better half to come with me and make a day out of it. She reluctantly agreed and we got a taxi up into the hills of Funchal where their stadium was located.

A taxi was a great idea, as the climb would have been virtually impossible in the heat. We got there in decent time and saw that next to the stadium was a fairly new training ground. It was named after Cristiano Ronaldo as apparently he had funded the building of it. Fair play to him as he's a god in Madiera. We headed to the ticket office and I requested two tickets for the centre of the main stand behind the dugouts. The cost was 8 euro each, for a Portuguese Premier Division game. Why are we so ripped off in England?

Tickets in hand, we headed to the bar. Another shock as a beer was only 1 euro. We even sampled some of the street food on offer, again not overly priced. We had a Panini of some sort with spicy sausage in it.

We were informed by the taxi driver to look out for the Nacional Ladies. These were a group of women who support the team, and sing along to all their songs whilst banging on a set of drums. I saw them alright, and I fucking heard them as well!! Ninety minutes of a high-pitched chant of 'Nacional' followed by boom boom boom on the drums.

The game was shit.... a 0-0 draw in front of 1500 fans. I'm glad I only paid 8 euro for it. The game started in bright sunshine but by the end, the clouds had started to roll in over the hills, and as we were quite high up, it was fairly chilly. Luckily, we warmed up when we got back to the all-inclusive drinks at the hotel.

14/7/17 – Tynecastle
Hearts v Newcastle

When Newcastle United announced a pre-season friendly against Heart of Midlothian at Tynecastle, I immediately booked train tickets to ensure I ticked off another ground.

The match was a Friday night game so we booked an early train to spend some time in Edinburgh. Paul and I decided to visit Easter Road, home of Hibernian. We hoped to take a look around before heading across the city to their biggest rivals, Hearts. We were allowed in to take a few photos, as well as the customary dugout photo. Hibs were scheduled to play the following day, however our return train was at 10pm that night so unfortunately we couldn't take in the game. Had I not been too hasty to buy cheap train tickets, we would have definitely have stayed for the second game.

Following that, a taxi ride through the endless amount of Edinburgh roadworks eventually saw us pull up to the three-sided Tynecastle stadium. We spoke a club host at reception, who showed us into the new area behind the scenes. This area had been created to include new changing rooms, as previously the old ones were located on the opposite side of the pitch in the stand which was currently being demolished and replaced. Once again, we got a dugout photo; however this area was also newly created from the seats in the stand, until the new ones are installed. We were then shown into the Hearts museum. Our guide gave us a quote; and its one which can be used for many clubs throughout the land, "we are a club with few trophies, but with loads of history".

Many of the items on display stem from the First World War when most of the first team players went off to fight, but not all of the players returned. Following this, we headed to the club's memorial garden. This is situated on one corner of the ground. It's a very moving area to visit, with numerous heart-shaped plaques adorning the walls, each with a personal note to loved ones who have sadly passed. There is also a statue of a 1914 soldier with a rifle over one arm, and a football in the other.

The game started off well with Dwight Gayle scoring after only three minutes. Hearts had the chance to level from the spot, but the penalty went high over the bar. They did level soon after but Gayle got his second to give us a half time lead.

The second half was a bit disjointed, mainly due to all the substitutions, and no further goals meant we won 2-1.

Paul and I had to leave as soon as the added-time board was held aloft as we had to make a mad dash to catch the last train. We made it with two minutes to spare.

1/8/18 – Estadio Municipal
SC Braga v Newcastle

As a birthday present to myself, as well as for completing The 92, I booked up to go to Portugal to see another pre-season kick-about in the sun.

I asked Singe if he was up for it and he said he was, so I started to make arrangements for this crazy trip. Newcastle were playing Porto three days before this game, and about 1000 toon fans booked up for that game. There is no direct flight from Newcastle to Porto so the prices from elsewhere soon rocketed. About two weeks after announcing the Porto game, the club confirmed a second match in the area against Braga. This time the prices were not too bad.

Singe and I got the train to Manchester Airport, arriving in enough time to see us down a few beers whilst waiting for our flight to Porto. Arriving in Porto late, we jumped on the tram to a stop near our hotel. The hotel was listed as one-star, and I'm not sure how it got that. The room was similar to a prison cell, but we just needed a place to sleep so it was good enough.

The following day we headed to the Estadio Do Dragao, home of FC Porto, for a stadium tour. It was quite a decent stadium and a decent way to kill some time. From there we headed by train to Braga. We arrived at our second hotel of the stay and it was a much better room than the previous night.

We went off to find a few town centre bars before heading to the ground. We were told by a few locals which way to go and everyone seemed friendly. When we arrived at the stadium, via this route we found this gate was locked and we would need to walk down to the main entrance. As the ground was built into a quarry this was quite a walk. Coupled with the fact it was 37 degrees, these two fat lads were sweating!

We eventually made it to the main entrance and bought our tickets. We then headed to the bar for a few beers. Singe got talking to Lee Ryder from The Chronicle, and soon we were being interviewed for Radio Newcastle back home.

The stadium was basically made up of two main stands with nothing behind each goal. It holds about 30,000 but there were only about 6,000 in there which included about 200 Newcastle fans. The first half saw an even game with both sides missing good chances. After the break though, Newcastle looked knackered, and Braga made them pay. Four unanswered goals were celebrated like it was a cup final by players and fans alike. The final whistle then saw a few half-hearted waves from the players to the travelling Geordies before trudging off down the tunnel. You're welcome!!

We headed out of the ground and up walk-way at the back of the goal carved into the rock. It was a decent vantage point for anyone not wanting to pay for tickets. We made our way up to our hotel stopping off at a local bar at around 10pm. The sweat was still pissing out of us, so the ice cold bottles of Super Bock were going down a treat.

The next morning was the return journey; and what a journey it turned out to be. We jumped on a bus from Braga for an hour-long ride which took us directly to Porto Airport. We got through customs and headed to the duty free. Singe bought himself a nice bottle of gin and we headed for Burger King. This is where the fun stopped. A delay of four hours is expected for the flight back to Manchester due to a problem with the aircraft. We were given a 5 euro voucher, which hardly covered the price of a coffee, for our inconvenience. With nothing else to do we simply lazed about in the airport till the hours ticked by. Eventually we took off, and as a small protest to Ryanair, we refrained from buying anything onboard.

When we arrived in Manchester we soon realised there were four other lads who had been to the game, and were unsure of how to get home. The flight delay had meant we had all missed our trains back home. We decided to stay together and challenge any train guard who questioned our story, as a group. Safety in numbers, I suppose. First was a train from the airport to Manchester Piccadilly. From there a train to Huddersfield, and then a third back to Chester le Street. We needn't have worried as not one ticket inspector was seen. We were collected at the station by my lovely wife Jackie, who even bought Singe and I a pizza for supper.

Printed in Great Britain
by Amazon